1819 & Before

The ISEAS – Yusof Ishak Institute (formerly Institute of Southeast Asian Studies) is an autonomous organization established in 1968. It is a regional centre dedicated to the study of socio-political, security, and economic trends and developments in Southeast Asia and its wider geostrategic and economic environment. The Institute's research programmes are grouped under Regional Economic Studies (RES), Regional Strategic and Political Studies (RSPS), and Regional Social and Cultural Studies (RSCS). The Institute is also home to the ASEAN Studies Centre (ASC), the Singapore APEC Study Centre, and the Temasek History Research Centre (THRC).

ISEAS Publishing, an established academic press, has issued more than 2,000 books and journals. It is the largest scholarly publisher of research about Southeast Asia from within the region. ISEAS Publishing works with many other academic and trade publishers and distributors to disseminate important research and analyses from and about Southeast Asia to the rest of the world.

1819 & Before

Singapore's Pasts

Edited by
Kwa Chong Guan

ISEAS YUSOF ISHAK
INSTITUTE

First published in Singapore in 2021 by
ISEAS Publishing
30 Heng Mui Keng Terrace
Singapore 119614

Email: publish@iseas.edu.sg
Website: bookshop.iseas.edu.sg

The responsibility for facts and opinions in this publication rests exclusively with the authors and their interpretations do not necessarily reflect the views or the policy of the publisher or its supporters.

ISEAS Library Cataloguing-in-Publication Data

Name(s): Kwa, Chong Guan, editor.
Title: 1819 and before : Singapore's pasts / edited by Kwa Chong Guan.
Description: Singapore : ISEAS–Yusof Ishak Institute, 2021. | Includes bibliographical references and index.
Identifiers: ISBN 9789814951111 (paperback) | ISBN 9789814951425 (pdf)
Subjects: LCSH: Singapore—History. | Singapore—Historiography.
Classification: LCC DS610.5 E34

Typeset by ISEAS Publishing
Printed in Singapore by Markono Print Media Pte Ltd

Endpapers: Drawing by Aaron Kao. This artist's impression depicts a variety of activities along the Singapore River circa fourteenth century. Archaeological evidence recovered around Empress Place suggests that a marketplace greeted seafarers as they sailed into the Singapore river. Its location offered shelter and swift transaction of goods. All that remained were mostly inorganic material such as trade stoneware, exquisite porcelain and ubiquitous earthenware and coins—their dense scatter was a testimony to a bustling riverbank, including a scuffle (centre bottom), which were not uncommon in port settlements, even in nineteenth-century Singapore. Unusual sandstone features may have been foundations for disintegrated timber structures that once served the maritime community. Unique artefact assemblages from different sites also indicated that urban planning delineated space use for commerce, residential and industries. By referencing ancient text descriptions, early modern illustrations, colonial photographs and ethnographical inferences, this image is an attempt to provide a plausible visualization of events that animated the shores of ancient Singapore.

Contents

Foreword

There is ample archaeological evidence today to argue that the island of Singapore was a trading port of significant importance from the fourteenth century, and perhaps earlier. This archaeological evidence has been accumulated over the decades from Singapore's very first archaeological dig in 1984 at Fort Canning Hill to the current work of the Archaeology Unit at the ISEAS – Yusof Ishak Institute. However, public interest in Singapore's pre-modern history is very much a recent phenomenon. For one, until recently historians paid very little attention to the island's pre-modern histories. As Kwa Chong Guan informs us in his first chapter in this volume, seminal texts like Mary Turnbull's *A History of Singapore, 1819–1975* did little to try to understand Singapore as a pre-1819 regional port or see it as part of the larger Malay world. Kwa notes that this was because there was either insufficient evidence of pre-1819 communities for serious investigation or that these communities were not believed to be significant enough to justify studying. Much of the writing of national histories in Southeast Asia took colonialism as the starting point and embarked on a chronology that included post–World War II decolonization, the emergence of postcolonial governments and their struggles to build new nations during the Cold War. Pre-modern empires, sea-faring communities and border-crossing fishermen did not command the same attention as newly formed nation-states, authoritarian governments and developing economies.

The other reason for the lack of interest in Singapore's pre-modern histories was decidedly ideological. Upon expulsion from Malaysia in 1965, Singapore's multicultural society made it politically untenable for its national history to be hitched to the civilization and culture of any particular ethnic group. With multiculturalism and meritocracy as its pillars, it would have been contradictory to equate national identity and culture with the country's largest ethnic community. In cutting the Gordian knot, the postcolonial government decided that the arrival of Sir Stamford Raffles to establish a British Station on Singapore would be ground zero without appeal to any ethnic culture. For many generations of Singaporeans, Singapore was born as a modern entity, transformed from the proverbial quiet fishing village to a colonial entrepôt with the stroke of a pen on 6 February 1819. This popular version of history was a strategic rupture, effectively dislocating the island from its surroundings and region, to introduce the island as *tabula rasa*.

Fast forward fifty years and the external environment has changed. Today the rise of China has made regionalism and sub-regionalism in Southeast Asia more geopolitically crucial than ever before. Southeast Asia's rapid growth has made it a region of opportunity, prompting Singapore leaders to encourage younger Singaporeans to develop a deeper understanding of the nearby countries. On the scholarly front, academics in the fields of history and archaeology have demonstrated the networks and linkages of the island to the region over the centuries prior to 1819. Key texts like *Seven Hundred Years: A History of Singapore* by Kwa Chong Guan, Derek Heng, Peter Borschberg and Tan Tai Yong and *Studying Singapore before 1800* edited by Kwa Chong Guan and Peter Borschberg bring together a body of evidence to show Singapore's pre-modern connectivity to the region vis-à-vis the economic activities of communities living on and around the island long before the arrival of Raffles.

The essays collected in this volume are summaries of a series of lectures organized by the ISEAS – Yusof Ishak Institute in the first half of 2019 as its contribution to commemorating the bicentennial of Stamford Raffles's arrival in Singapore. Colleagues of the former Nalanda-Sriwijaya Centre were invited to speak on how their research contributed to a major theme of the bicentennial, inviting Singaporeans to reflect on Singapore's longer seven-hundred-year history.

I would like to thank my colleagues for accepting our invitation to speak on how their work pushes and probes the frontiers of our understanding of our history before Raffles. The summaries of their lectures compiled in this volume provide a glimpse of how deeply connected our history is to that of the long cycles of the maritime histories of the region and the importance of the Malay world to Singapore's identity and place in the region. *1819 & Before: Singapore's Pasts* will, I am confident, form a basis for future research on Singapore's pre-modern history and the island's changing roles under the Śrīvijaya Empire and the Majapahit Empire, followed by the Malacca and Johor Sultanates, and how Singapore has always been shaped by its surroundings. The Nalanda-Sriwijaya Centre has bequeathed its successor, the Temasek History Research Centre, a substantive legacy of scholarship to draw upon for its research.

I would like to thank my ISEAS – Yusof Ishak Institute colleagues for organizing the series of lectures that forms the basis of this book. I am also grateful to Tan Chin Tiong, former Director of ISEAS and current Senior Advisor, as well as Choi Shing Kwok, current Director, for supporting this project.

Terence Chong
Deputy Director
ISEAS

Acknowledgments

The essays gathered here are revisions and summaries of a series of lectures convened by the former Nalanda-Sriwijaya Centre in 2019 to commemorate the Bicentennial of Stamford Raffles's landing in Singapore. I thank Terence Chong, Deputy Director of ISEAS, for inviting me to help plan and coordinate the series of lectures and to edit their revised summaries for publication. I am also grateful to Tan Chin Tiong, former Director of ISEAS and current Senior Advisor, for supporting this project.

I would like to thank current and former staff, fellows and affiliates of the Nalanda-Sriwijaya Centre for accepting the invitation to speak on how their research relates to and probes and challenges our understanding of Singapore's history before Raffles (or lack thereof). Their research provides a solid foundation for the Temasek History Research Centre to build upon.

The Public Affairs staff of ISEAS and the staff of the former Nalanda-Sriwijaya Centre organized the lectures with their usual efficiency, so leaving me the pleasant duty of moderating the lectures. Ms Fong Sok Eng has provided stalwart service in organizing the lectures and coordinating the publication of this volume.

Special thanks and appreciation to Terence Chong, as then Head of the Nalanda-Sriwijaya Centre and now Head of the Temasek History Research Centre, for continuing to support publication of this collection of essays.

Contributors

Kwa Chong Guan

Kwa Chong Guan is a Senior Fellow at the S. Rajaratnam School of International Studies, Nanyang Technological University, where he is currently working on issues of crisis management and risk mitigation of regional security issues. As Associate Fellow at the Temasek History Research Centre and Adjunct (Hon.) Associate Professor at the History Department, National University of Singapore, he is interested in the connected histories of monsoon Asia. Kwa chairs the Archaeology Advisory Panel established by the National Heritage Board in August 2019.

John N. Miksic

John N. Miksic received his BA from Dartmouth College, MA from Ohio University and PhD from Cornell University based on archaeological fieldwork on a trading port of the eleventh to thirteenth centuries in Sumatra. He has worked in Malaysia as a Peace Corps volunteer teacher and agricultural extension worker, in Sumatra as a rural development advisor under USAID, and at Gadjah Mada University, Yogyakarta for six years under a grant from the Ford Foundation and the Asian Cultural Council. In 1987 he moved to the National University of Singapore, where he is Emeritus Professor in the Southeast Asian Studies Department. He has been affiliated with the Department of History, University Scholars Programme and Asia Research Institute. He founded the Archaeology Unit at the ISEAS – Yusof Ishak Institute. He received a Special Recognition Award and the Pingat Bakti Setia long-service award from the government of Singapore, and the title Kanjeng Raden Harya Temenggung from the Susuhunan of Surakarta (Indonesia).

His book *Singapore and the Silk Road of the Sea* won the inaugural award for best book on Singapore history in 2018. His specialties are the historical archaeology of Southeast Asia, urbanization, trade, Buddhism and ceramics.

Derek Heng

Derek Heng is currently Professor and Department Chair at the Department of History, Northern Arizona University. He was Associate Professor of Humanities and Head of Studies (History) at Yale-NUS College and was previously Head of NSC from January 2014 to July 2015. He specializes in the trans-regional history of Maritime Southeast Asia and the South China Sea during the first and early second millennia AD, and is the author of *Sino-Malay Trade and Diplomacy in the Tenth through the Fourteenth Century* (Athens: Ohio University Press, 2009) and co-author of *Seven Hundred Years: A History of Singapore* (Singapore: National Library Board, 2019). He has also authored a number of journal articles and book chapters on the Chinese material remains recovered from archaeological sites in Southeast Asia, as well as having edited three volumes on the history and historiography of Singapore's past. He is currently working on methods in integrating archaeological data from Southeast Asia with Chinese digital textual databases. He maintains a keen interest on the historiography of Singapore, and he has edited *New Perspectives and Sources on the History of Singapore: A Multi-Disciplinary Approach* (Singapore: National Library Board, 2006), *Reframing Singapore: Memory, Identity and Trans-Regionalism,* ICAS Series volume 6 (Amsterdam: Amsterdam University Press, 2009) and *Singapore in Global History* (Amsterdam: Amsterdam University Press, 2011).

Michael Flecker

Michael Flecker, Managing Director of Maritime Explorations, has overseen some of the most important shipwreck excavations in Asia over the past thirty years. They include the ninth-century *Belitung* (Tang), twelfth-century *Flying Fish*, thirteenth-century *Java Sea*, fifteenth-century *Bakau*, c.1608 *Binh Thuan* and c.1690 *Vung Tau* wrecks. He earned his PhD from the National University of Singapore based on the excavation of the tenth-century *Intan Wreck*, and he specializes in ancient Asian ship construction and maritime trade. He has twice been a Visiting Fellow at the Nalanda-Sriwijaya Centre and is presently a Visiting Fellow at the Archaeology Unit, ISEAS – Yusof Ishak Institute.

Leonard Y. Andaya

Leonard Y. Andaya received his BA from Yale University and his MA and PhD from Cornell University. He is at present Professor of Southeast

Asian History at the University of Hawai'i, and has written extensively on the early modern period, particularly of Indonesia and Malaysia. His most recent publications are *Leaves of the Same Tree: Trade and Ethnicity in the Straits of Melaka* (Honolulu: University of Hawai'i Press, 2008), (with Barbara Watson Andaya) *A History of Early Modern Southeast Asia* (Cambridge: Cambridge University Press, 2015) and (with Barbara Watson Andaya) *A History of Malaysia*, third edition (London: Palgrave, 2017). He was the Tan Chin Tuan Professor in Malay Studies at NUS in 2011–12 and the inaugural holder of the Yusof Ishak Chair in the Social Sciences at NUS in 2017–18.

Andrea Acri

Andrea Acri (PhD Leiden University, 2011) is Assistant Professor in Tantric Studies at the École Pratique des Hautes Études (PSL University, Paris) and Associate Fellow at the Temasek History Research Centre (formerly known as the Nalanda-Sriwijaya Centre). He has held various research and teaching positions in India, Singapore, the Netherlands and Australia. He has authored articles in international academic journals and published edited volumes on Shaiva and Buddhist tantric traditions in South and Southeast Asia, as well as wider cultural and historical dynamics of Intra-Asian connectivity. His monograph *Dharma Pātañjala*, which originally appeared in the Gonda Indological Studies Series (Egbert Forsten/Brill, 2011), has been recently republished in India by Aditya Prakashan (New Delhi, 2017) and in Indonesian translation by EFEO/KPG Gramedia (Jakarta, 2018).

Iain Sinclair

Iain Sinclair is an Honorary Research Fellow at the University of Queensland School of Historical and Philosophical Inquiry. He studies the history, art and religion of South and Southeast Asia using primary sources in classical languages. His PhD dissertation (Monash University, 2016) examined the advent of tantrism in the medieval monasteries of the Kathmandu Valley. His recent publications include "Traces of the Cholas in Old Singapura" in *Sojourners to Settlers—Tamils in Southeast Asia and Singapore*, volume 1, edited by Nalina Gopal and Arun Mahizhnan (Singapore: Indian Heritage Centre and Institute for Policy Studies, 2019), "Sanskritic Buddhism as an Asian Universalism" in *Imagining Asia(s)* edited by Andrea Acri et al. (Singapore: ISEAS – Yusof Ishak Institute, 2019) and "Coronation and Liberation according to a Javanese Monk in China" in *Esoteric Buddhism in Mediaeval Maritime Asia* edited by Andrea Acri (Singapore: ISEAS – Yusof Ishak Institute, 2016). He has been a Visiting Fellow at the Nalanda-Sriwijaya Centre and a Käte Hamburger Kolleg Fellow at the Centre for Religious Studies, Ruhr University Bochum.

Peter Borschberg

Peter Borschberg teaches history at NUS. He has authored several studies on pre-1800 Singapore and the Straits region, including *The Singapore and Melaka Straits: Violence, Security and Diplomacy in the 17th Century* (2010), *Singapore in the Cycles of the Longue Durée* (JMBRAS, 2017) and *The Port of Singapore c.1290–1819: Evidence, Frameworks and Challenges* (JMBRAS, 2018).

Tai Yew Seng

Tai Yew Seng is a Visiting Fellow at the Temasek History Research Centre and a ceramic archaeologist who specializes in excavating and handling ceramic from kiln sites, shipwrecks, ruins and tombs. He also has expertise in the Southeast Asian maritime trade with China. At ISEAS he conducted research on Singapore's pre-modern history and Chinese navigation charts and texts. During his stint as a Research Fellow at the Earth Observatory of Singapore, Nanyang Technological University (NTU), he participated in the Aceh Geohazard Project, which involved the collection and analysis of ancient ceramic sherds from over forty-four villages. Dr Tai has also taught several courses on Chinese culture and material culture at the Chinese Department at NTU and the National University of Singapore. He has published a number of research papers and co-authored books on ceramic archaeology and maritime trade in English and Chinese.

Aaron Kao

Aaron Kao joined the ISEAS Archaeology Unit as Research Officer. He majored in painting and received his diploma (as the top graduate from the school of Fine Art) from Lasalle SIA College of the Arts in 1999. As a scholarship recipient, he received his Bachelor of Arts degree (with Distinction) from Royal Melbourne Institute of Technology in 2003 and is currently pursuing postgraduate studies in archaeology at the University of Oxford under the Tun Dato Sir Cheng-Lock Tan MA Scholarship.

He was introduced to Singapore archaeology when he joined the Fort Serapong project in 2006. That experience exposed him to the world of archaeology and his interest blossomed to encompass the pre-modern history of Singapore and the region. He has since participated in numerous excavations in Singapore and was also part of the team for ISEAS's field school projects in Cambodia and Indonesia.

Apart from doing fieldwork and post-excavation processing, Aaron also applies his fine art training as illustrator for the Archaeology Unit. His main research interests are Singapore earthenware and its maritime cultural landscape. He has published a conference paper with SEAMEO-SPAFA International Conference on Southeast Asian Archaeology.

1

Introduction: Approaches to Singapore's Past before 1819

Kwa Chong Guan

Singapore commemorated the bicentennial of Thomas Stamford Raffles's establishment of a British station on this island with a year-long series of blockbuster exhibitions and accompanying international conferences and ground-up events involving community and volunteer efforts. In contrast to the centennial of Raffles's arrival in Singapore, which was a celebration of the achievements of the Crown Colony that had grown out of the British station Raffles established, the bicentennial was a commemoration inviting Singaporeans to reflect on the two hundred years of their island's past in the long cycles of the preceding five hundred years of time. For many, this invitation was a challenge, as the prevailing and dominant public narrative of Singapore was that it had only a two-hundred-year history.

This template of Singapore having a two-hundred-year history started by Raffles was laid down by Raffles himself. On 8 January 1819, Raffles reported to Governor-General Hastings that his inquiries at Pinang indicated that Singapore "has been deserted for Centuries and long before the Dutch power existed in these Seas".[1] British colonial officials from Dr John Crawfurd (1783–1868) have confirmed this. The template was consolidated by generations of historians, from Raffles Professor of History Kennedy G. Tregonning and his colleagues at the History Department of the old University of Singapore in the 1960s through to the 1990s.

Crawfurd, as the second Resident of Singapore after William Farquhar, would be in a position to authoritatively state that "for a period of about five centuries and a half, there is no record of Singapore having been occupied, and it was only the occasional resort of pirates. In that year [1811], it was taken possession of by the party from whom we [the British] first received it, an officer of the government of Johore called the Tumângung. This person told me himself that he came there with about 150 followers, a few months before the British expedition which afterwards captured Java passed the island, and this happened in the summer of 1811."[2]

L.A. Mills was the first to establish the founding of Singapore as the beginning of a history of British Malaya, 1824–67.[3] His work became a basic text for a new generation of historians trained at the History Department of the new University of Malaya established in 1949. They were taught that the history of Malaya was all contained in the records of the Straits Settlement archived in the old Raffles Library and the 273 series of Colonial Office Records.[4] Raffles Professor of History K.G. Tregonning summed up the underlying assumption of the research of the department in an essay commemorating Singapore's sesquicentennial: "Modern Singapore began in 1819. Nothing that occurred on the island prior to this has particular relevance to an understanding of the contemporary scene; it is of antiquarian interest only."[5]

Fifty years on we are looking to well before 1819 for Singapore's beginnings, and reflect on its relevance for Singapore today. That we can do this is because of three breakthroughs in approaching Singapore history. These are, first, a breakthrough into the archaeology of fourteenth-century Singapore; second, a breakthrough in re-reading of the *Malay Annals*, or *Sulalatus-Salatin*; and third, a breakthrough into the early modern Portuguese, Dutch and other records and archives. Each of these breakthroughs was associated with or led by staff, fellows and affiliates of the old Nalanda-Sriwijaya Centre, and now the Temasek History Research Centre. The commemoration of Singapore's bicentennial was an occasion to convene some of these staff, fellows and affiliates to share their research in enabling these three breakthroughs to approaching Singapore's pre-1800 past.

The Archaeological Breakthrough

The old National Museum was in 1984 able, with funding support from the Shell companies in Singapore, to invite John N. Miksic, then lecturing on archaeology at Gadjah Mada University, Jogjakarta, to undertake an archaeological investigation of Fort Canning for any artefacts of the historic remains both Raffles and Crawfurd saw in 1819–22. Against the odds, a two-week survey and excavation recovered *in situ* fourteenth-century artefacts, indicating that there may be much more to be recovered through further excavations.[6]

Thirty-five years of further excavations by Miksic and his team of volunteers on not only Fort Canning but its environs have recovered several tons of ceramic, stoneware and earthenware sherds[7] as confirming evidence of the *Sulalatus-Salatin* claim that Singapura was "a great city to which foreigners resorted in great numbers so that the fame of the city and its greatness spread throughout the world."[8]

The wide range and large volume of artefacts recovered is evidence of Temasek/Singapura's dense and intricate networks of trade in the region, into the Chinese market and also across the Bay of Bengal. Derek Heng has been drawing on the archaeological data to situate Temasek/Singapura as a regional and international trading port in the thirteenth and fourteenth centuries.[9] Marine archaeology of shipwrecks and their cargoes[10] provides us today a new understanding of the ships and volume of trade then being shipped around the region,[11] as Flecker shows in his essay.[12] Altogether, the archaeological evidence indicates that Temasek/Singapura's survival and prosperity in the fourteenth century was as dependent upon the viability of its trade networks and cycles of trade in China and across the Indian Ocean as is the case today. These excavations were, however, not part of a planned archaeology research programme, but were essentially rescue or salvage archaeology to excavate and recover archaeological materials and data from sites as they were slated for urban redevelopment. It is to the credit of Miksic and his team that they were able to rise to the occasion to undertake these salvage archaeology excavations of a site before its redevelopment and manage the subsequent minimal conservation of the artefacts recovered and documentation of the site excavated. They achieved this without much institutional support from the museums for archaeological research.

Only in 2010 was an Archaeological Unit headed by Miksic set up as a component of the Nalanda-Sriwijaya Centre, which was established in the preceding year to pursue research on the historical interactions among Asian societies and civilizations. Archaeology was promoted as one way to investigate these historical interactions between Asian civilizations. Today, the Archaeology Unit is actively coordinating further excavations in Singapore[13] and promoting greater awareness of archaeology and the challenges it faces[14] via various public outreach programmes.

A Breakthrough in Re-Reading the *Sulalatus-Salatin*

The first six chapters of the *Sulalatus-Salatin* on the genealogy of the Melaka sultans are, in Sir Richard Winstedt's view, a "hotchpotch of Chola and Palembang folklore [out of which] little can be made."[15] For Winstedt, this dismissal of not only the *Sulalatus-Salatin* but much else of classical Malay literature is grounded on a binary distinction rooted in Greek philosophy between *mythos*, referring to fable, folklore and fiction, and *logos*, rational argument founded on evidence. Consequently, the account of Singapura receiving its name from a roving prince from Palembang arriving at Temasek where he espied what he was told was a "singa" and decided it was a good omen to settle on the island has been dismissed as fiction and myth. By now, more than one generation of students of Malay language and literature have struggled to break this Eurocentric framing of classical Malay literature as more romance and *mythos* than *logos* and history.[16]

Oliver W. Wolters, a former Malayan Civil Service officer turned academic historian, published in 1970 a rather underappreciated study on *The Fall of Śrīvijaya in Malay History* connecting the deep vertical intertextuality of the *mythos* of the *Sulalatus-Salatin*'s genealogy of the founder of Melaka to the Buddhist symbolism of Sri Tribuana as the Lord of the Three Worlds and his consecration (*abhiṣeka*) as a Bodhisattva to claim the legacy of Śrīvijaya for Melaka.[17] That Śrīvijaya was not only a major emporium but also a major centre of Buddhist learning is well established.

The former Nalanda-Sriwijaya Centre, as its name indicated, was established in large part to further explore the historical interactions underpinning the centrality of maritime Southeast Asia and Śrīvijaya in the Buddhist world spanning Xian to Nalanda.[18] The network of Buddhist masters, texts and icons across the Buddhist world of maritime Southeast Asia, as we are now recognizing from research that emanated from the Nalanda-Sriwijaya Centre, led in large part by its founding head Sen Tansen[19] and by Andrea Acri, was esoteric Buddhist,[20] and not, as in mainstream understanding, Mahayana until the thirteenth-century conversion to the Theravada tradition.

Tun Bambang, the scribe of the 1612 CE copy of the *Sulalatus-Salatin* known to us as Raffles MS 18, was probably unaware of these deep Buddhist tropes to the founder of Melaka. Acri, in his contribution to this volume, unravels yet another Buddhist trope in the *Sulalatus-Salatin* story of Sri Tribuana jettisoning his crown to save his ship sinking in a storm while sailing to Temasek. Iain Sinclair's essay in this volume digs deeper into the lion motif that has become a brand name for Singapore today.[21] The name Singapura, as these contributions show, is rooted in deep Esoteric/Tantric Buddhist tropes that not too many of us today are aware of.

Another dimension of the *Sulalatus-Salatin*'s narrative of Malay history is the role of the sea nomads. Leonard Andaya in his contribution to this volume examines the *Sulalatus-Salatin* references to the undivided loyalty of these sea nomad communities to the Sultans of Melaka and Johor to conclude that these *orang laut*, marginalized as isolated tribal groups in the nineteenth century, played a central role in the making of the *negara selat* in earlier centuries.[22]

An Archival Breakthrough

John Crawfurd was clear that the island of Singapore was "only the occasional resort of pirates" for the five hundred years from the time of the abandonment of the settlement he saw the remains of in 1822 until the arrival of Raffles. According to Raffles Professor of History Tregonning, the Portuguese capture of Melaka in 1511 and the guerrilla war they were engaged in against Sultan Mahmud seeking to recapture Melaka, their expeditions up the Johor River to take out an incipient Johor sultanate, and confronting the Dutch challenge for control of the waters around Singapore did not affect Singapore and the region, if at all. In a 1958 feature article in the *Straits Times*, Tregonning wrote that "Asia, not the European in Asia, must be our theme, and suddenly, if you think of that, it makes the Portuguese and the Dutch most insignificant, and almost extraneous", that "they were a few heretical fish in a Muslim sea, and … they did not affect Asia much at all. Rather the contrary, Asia profoundly affected them."[23] Tregonning's young colleague at the History Department, Ian A. Macgregor, decided to take on the challenge of researching the Portuguese in Malaya, and especially in Johor. The four articles[24] he managed to complete before his unexpected death were instrumental in framing the archaeological investigations of Johor Lama lead by C.A. Gibson-Hill and a team from the old Raffles Museum in the mid-1950s.[25] Unfortunately, these two early forays by Macgregor and Gibson-Hill into the Portuguese and other early modern records for what can be inferred from them about Singapore were not followed up. Tregonning dismissed Gibson-Hill's work and that of the *Journal of the Malayan Branch of the Royal Asiatic Society* as being only of antiquarian interest.

There was no further search for and study of early modern Portuguese and Dutch records of Singapore history before 1800 until the mid-1990s, when Peter Borschberg was led to look into the Dutch archives by his studies of the seventeenth-century Dutch jurist Hugo Grotius's engagement by the Dutch East India Company to defend their seizure of the Portuguese carrack off Changi against charges of freebooting. Borschberg's research into the seizure of the Santa Catarina broadened into studying seventeenth-century Luso-Dutch rivalry in the Straits of Melaka and Singapore, the seascapes on which that rivalry played out,[26] and the role of these Chartered Companies as instruments of empires in Asia in the construction of an increasingly connected global history from 1500 CE.[27] From Borschberg's searching of the early modern Portuguese, Spanish and Dutch archives and records emerges an earlier alternative understanding of Singapore's strategic location,[28] in contrast to the Tregonning framing of Singapore's strategic location within the world of the East India Company and its attempts to secure the China trade. Borschberg's contribution to this volume acknowledges the pioneering work of Macgregor and Gibson-Hill before outlining the challenges of accessing the Portuguese and Dutch records for Singapore before 1800.

Conclusion

"To write a history of the old Singapura", according to C.O. Blagden in 1919,[29] "would be something like the task imposed upon the children of Israel by the Pharaoh: for where should one seek the straw to make those bricks with?" A century later there are more bundles of straw to make the bricks for the construction of a history of Singapore. Digital technology is enabling us to more effectively access classical Chinese textual records on Malaya and Singapore,[30] and so increasing our "bundles of straw" to make the bricks to construct our pre-1819 history. The contributions to this volume outline the new data from archaeological investigations and investigations of the early modern Portuguese and Dutch archives.

The problem of making sense of these texts, locating the toponyms in these texts, and chronologically sequencing the occupation of that name place that confronted Blagden[31] continues to challenge us today. Blagden could not locate the landmarks on the Mao Kun map that guided Admiral Zheng He when he sailed past Danmaxi. J.V. Mills spent some forty years studying the Mao Kun map to fix these place names to determine whether the admiral sailed his fleet through the narrow Keppel Harbour passageway or the wider main strait.[32] Today, a new generation of scholars,[33] represented by Tai Yew Seng in this volume, is studying anew the Mao Kun map and the other classical Chinese textual references to Singapore.

A major challenge confronting any writing of Singapore's history prior to 1819 is its connection and relevance to Singapore's history after 1819. Blagden did not attempt to make any connection between the section he wrote on "Singapore prior to 1819" in the chapter on the historical background of Singapore in *One Hundred Years of Singapore* to the following section he also wrote on "the foundation of the settlement" by Raffles. That section continues and merges well into Roland St. J. Braddell's contribution on "A short history of the Colony".

The disconnect between the history of Singapore before and after the arrival of Raffles was emphasized by Tregonning and his colleague C.M. Turnbull in her benchmark textbook on *A History of Singapore*. Admittedly, none of the historical evidence from the breakthroughs in approaching Singapore before 1800 was available to Turnbull when she wrote the first edition of her book in 1975. But she was fully aware of these breakthroughs in our understanding of Singapore before Raffles when she revised her book for its final edition in 2009, and was clear in dismissing these breakthroughs: "The findings of careful archaeological work carried out in the late twentieth century at Fort Canning and near the Singapore River, together with a study of pre-colonial records, charts and maps, supplement but basically support the previously known story; namely that Temasek appeared and flourished for a few decades as one of a number of moderately prosperous ports in the region but came to a sudden, violent and mysterious end at the close of the fourteenth century, when its ruler fled to found the more successful Melaka ... the thorough investigations of the late twentieth century confirm that, after the fall of Temasek, nothing of significance took place on the island until Raffles's party landed in 1819."[34]

The Singapore bicentennial, although not labelled as such, was in effect a massive exercise in public history reaching out to engage Singaporeans to review and rethink a foundational event in Singapore's history. The former Nalanda-Sriwijaya Centre, during the ten years of its existence, contributed much to facilitating this review and rethinking of Singapore's past leading to Raffles's arrival in Singapore. It leaves a solid foundation of research for the new Temasek History Research Centre to build upon and further our understanding of the Temasek era of Singapore's history.

Notes

1. Raffles to Hastings quoted in J. Bastin, *Raffles and Hastings: Private Exchanges behind the Founding of Singapore* (Singapore: National Library Board/Marshall Cavendish, 2014), p. 14.

2. J. Crawfurd, *A Descriptive Dictionary of the Indian Islands & Adjacent Countries* (1856; repr., Kuala Lumpur/Singapore: Oxford in Asia Historical Reprints, 1971), *sub voca* "Singapore" at p. 402.

3. Mills, "British Malaya 1824–1867, Edited for Reprinting with a Bibliography of Writings in English on British Malaya, 1786–1867", *Journal of the Malayan Branch of the Royal Asiatic Society* 33, no. 3 (1960).

4. Kwa Chong Guan and Ho Chi Tim, "Archival Records in the Writing of Singapore History: A Perspective from the Archives", in *The Makers & Keepers of Singapore History*, edited by Loh Kah Seng and Lai Kai Khiun (Singapore: Ethos Books/Singapore Heritage Society, 2010), pp. 48–66.

5. K.G. Tregonning, "Historical Background", in *Modern Singapore*, edited by Ooi Jin-bee and Chiang Hai Ding (Singapore: University of Singapore Press, 1969), p. 14.

6. J.N. Miksic, *Archaeological Research on the "Forbidden Hill" of Singapore: Excavations at Fort Canning 1984* (Singapore: National Museum 1985). See also Miksic's more personal recollections and reflections of that excavation in his "Singapore's Archaeological Heritage: What Has Been Saved?", in *Rethinking Cultural Resource Management in Southeast Asia: Preservation, Development, and Neglect*, edited by J.N. Miksic et al. (London: Anthem, 2011), pp. 217–34.

7. J.N. Miksic, *Singapore and the Silk Road of the Sea, 1300–1800* (Singapore: NUS Press, 2013) is a summation of some twenty years of excavations.

8. Quoted from the C.C. Brown translation, "Sejarah Melayu: A Translation of Raffles MS 18 (in the Library of the R.A.S., London)", *Journal of the Malayan Branch of the Royal Asiatic Society* 35 nos. 2–3 (1952): 31.

9. D. Heng, "Temasik as an International and Regional Trading Port in the Thirteenth and Fourteenth Centuries", *Journal of the Malaysian Branch of the Royal Asiatic Society* 72, no. 1 (1999) 113–24; also his "Situating Temasik within the Larger Regional Context: Maritime Asia and Malay State Formation in the Pre-Modern era", in *Singapore in Global History*, edited by D. Heng and Syed Muhd. Khairudin Aljunied (Amsterdam: Amsterdam University Press, 2011), pp. 27–50.

10. D. Heng, "Ships, Shipwrecks, and Archaeological Recoveries as Sources of Southeast Asian History", in Oxford Research Encyclopedias, Asian History, edited by D. Luddens (Oxford University Press, 2018), https://doi.org/10.1093/acrefore/9780190277727.013.97.

11. Kwa Chong Guan, "Locating Singapore on the Maritime Silk Road: Evidence from Maritime Archaeology, Ninth to Early Nineteenth Centuries", Nalanda-Sriwijaya Centre Working Paper no. 10 (January 2012).

12. See also Michael Flecker, "Early Voyaging in the South China Sea: Implications on Territorial Claims", Nalanda-Sriwijaya Centre Working Paper no. 19 (August 2015).

13. Lim Chen Sian, "Preliminary Report on the Archaeological Investigations at the National Gallery Singapore", Nalanda-Sriwijaya Centre Archaeology Report Series no. 5 (January 2017); Lim Chen Sian, "Preliminary Report on the Archaeological Investigations at the Victoria Concert Hall", Nalanda-Sriwijaya Centre Archaeology Report Series no. 9 (January 2019).

14. Lim Chen Sian, Duncan H. Brown, D. Heng, Frank M. Meddens, and J.N. Miksic, "Archiving Archaeological Materials", Nalanda-Sriwijaya Centre Archaeology Unit Archaeology Report Series no. 7 (December 2017); also

M. Flecker, *Legislation on Underwater Cultural Heritage in Southeast Asia: Evolution and Outcomes*, Trends in Southeast Asia no. 23/2017 (Singapore: ISEAS – Yusof Ishak Institute, 2017).

15. R. Winstedt, *A History of Malaya*, rev. ed. (Singapore: Marican & Sons, 1962), p. 41.

16. For example, Ahmat Adam, *Antara Sejarah dan Mitos: Sejarah Melayu & Hang Tuah dalam Historiografi Malaysia* (Petaling Jaya: Strategic Information and Research Development Centre, 2016).

17. O.W. Wolters, *The Fall of Śrīvijaya in Malay History* (London: Lund Humphries; Kuala Lumpur: Oxford University, 1970). Kwa Chong Guan, "Singapura as a Central Place in Malay History and Identity", in *Singapore from Temasek to the 21st Century: Reinventing the Global City*, edited by Karl Hack and Jean-Louis Margolin, with Karine Delaye (Singapore: NUS Press, 2010), pp. 133–54.

18. The contested heritage of Nalanda Mahavihara, revived in 2010 as Nalanda University, is examined in the essays in *Records, Recoveries, Remnants and Inter-Asian Interconnections: Decoding Cultural Heritage*, edited by Anjana Sharma (Singapore: ISEAS – Yusof Ishak Institute, 2018).

19. Tansen Sen, "Buddhism and the Maritime Crossings", in *China and beyond in the Medieval Period: Cultural Crossings and Inter-regional Connections*, edited by D.C. Wong and G. Heldt (New Delhi: Manohar for Cambria Press and NSC ISEAS, 2014), pp. 39–62; also Tansen Sen, "Maritime Southeast Asia between South Asia and China to the Sixteenth Century", *TRaNS: Trans-Regional and -National Studies of Southeast Asia* 2, no. 1 (2014), pp. 31–50.

20. A. Acri, ed., *Esoteric Buddhism in Medieval Maritime Asia: Networks of Masters, Texts, Icons* (Singapore: ISEAS – Yusof Ishak Institute, 2016); also A. Acri, "The Place of Nusantara in the Sanskritic Buddhist Cosmopolis", *TRaNS* 6, no. 2 (2018), 139–65.

21. Note also his "Sang Sapurba/Maulivarmadeva, First of the Last Indo-Malay Kings", *NSC Highlights* 12 (May 2019), pp. 6–8.

22. L. Andaya, *Leaves of the Same Tree: Trade and Ethnicity in the Straits of Melaka* (Honolulu: University of Hawai'i Press, 2008), chapter 6 elaborates on the vital role of the *orang laut* in the maritime realm of the Malay sultans.

23. Tregonning, in "A New Approach to Malayan History", *Straits Times*, 21 November 1958, was taking to its logical conclusion the argument of the Dutch socio economic historian Jacob C. van Leur, who had written a series of polemical articles about the writing of Dutch East Indies history as a young Dutch colonial official in the 1930s, before he died in action during World War II. Van Leur argued that it was wrong to write the history of the East Indies as a part of Dutch history. Van Leur argued that there was an "autonomous" Asian world, and he called for the study of Asia's history from within that world. The posthumous publication of a selection of van Leur's writings in English in 1955 as *Indonesian Trade and Society: Essays in Asian Social and Economic History* (The Hague:

van Hoeve, 1955) started a historiographical controversy that reverberates to this day.

24. Not including a comprehensive survey of "Some Aspects of Portuguese Historical Writing of the Sixteenth and Seventeenth Centuries on South East Asia", in *Historians of South East Asia: Historical Writing on the Peoples of Asia*, edited by D.G.E. Hall (London: Oxford University Press, 1961), pp. 172–99,

25. I.A. Mcgregor, C.A. Gibson-Hill, and G. de G. Sieveking, "Papers on Johore Lama and the Portuguese in Malaya (1511–1641)", *Journal of the Malayan Branch of the Royal Asiatic Society* 28, no. 2 (1955).

26. P. Borschberg, *The Singapore and Melaka Straits: Violence, Security and Diplomacy in the 17th Century* (Singapore: NUS Press, 2010).

27. P. Borschberg, "Chartered Companies and Empire", in *Empire in Asia: A New Global History*, vol. 1, *From Chinggisid to Qing*, edited by J. Fairey and B.P. Farrell (London: Bloomsbury Academic, 2018), pp. 269–94. Sanjay Subrahmanyam leads the argument for connected histories of Asia; see for example his *Empires between Islam & Christianity, 1500–1800* (Delhi: Permanent Black; New York: SUNY Press, 2019).

28. Borschberg's "Singapore's Longer History", *Jahrbuch für Europäische Übereegeschichte* 19 (2019), elaborates on issues of Singapore's "strategic location" in its longer history.

29. In his essay "Singapore Prior to 1819" for the volume celebrating the centennial of Singapore's founding, *One Hundred Years of Singapore*, edited by Walter Makepeace et al. (1921; repr., Singapore: Oxford University Press 1991), pp. 1–5.

30. See D. Heng, "Premodern Island-Southeast Asian History in the Digital Age: Opportunities and Challenges through Chinese Textual Database Research", *Bijdragen tot de Taal-, Land- en Volkenkunde* 175 (2019): 29–57 on new ways of accessing the Chinese texts today.

31. C.O. Blagden, "Notes on Malay history", *Journal of the Straits Branch of the Royal Asiatic Society* no. 53 (1909), pp. 139–62.

32. J.V. Mills, *Ma Huan*; Ying-yai Sheng-lan, *The Overall Survey of the Ocean's Shores* [1433], Hakluyt Society Extra Series no. 42 (Cambridge: University Press, 1970), appendix 2, "The Mao K'un Map", pp. 236–303.

33. Geoffrey Gobble, "Maritime Southeast Asia: The View from Tang-Song China", Nalanda-Sriwijaya Centre Working Paper Series no. 16 (May 2014).

34. Turnbull, *A History of Modern Singapore 1819–2005* (Singapore, NUS Press, 2009), p. 4.

2

Issues and Approaches to Studying Singapore before 1819

John N. Miksic

Archaeological research began in Singapore in 1984. Since then, over half a million artefacts have been recovered from systematic excavations. These remains fall into two periods: the Temasek era (fourteenth to sixteenth century) and the Singapore era (1819 to the present). Historical sources from the seventeenth and eighteenth centuries demonstrate that during this time Singapore was still a source of maritime manpower for rulers vying to control the local waterways, and that ships took on provisions here,[1] but the only artefacts on land that date from this 200-year period are two ceramic sherds excavated at St. Andrew's Cathedral.

The artefacts from excavations are reliable proof that Singapore was home to a sophisticated multicultural society with a complex set of links to local and long-distance trade before 1350. Although these basic outlines of ancient Singapore are now clear, there are still important questions about Singapore's history that further research, including work in laboratories and archives, may be able to answer. The important questions concern the provenance of artefacts, many of which were not made locally but were imported; the nature of Singapore's ancient ecology and environment; reconstruction of artefacts; statistical analysis of intra-site variation; and comparisons with other sites in the region.

Texts, Legends and Surface Finds

The Malay Annals

The pre-colonial artefacts from Singapore confirm the hypothesis that Singapore in the fourteenth century corresponded closely to the way it was depicted in the *Malay Annals* as a bustling multi-ethnic port.[2] The *Malay Annals* are not entirely reliable as a historical source; they were compiled for a political purpose, to support the claims of the Malay royal family who ruled Melaka in the mid-fifteenth century, when Islam replaced esoteric Buddhism as the main religion in the court. Numerous recensions of the *Malay Annals* exist; the oldest version, and the one probably closest to the original, is known as the *Raffles MS 18*. This was composed in Johor in the early seventeenth century, apparently just after Singapore had been devastated by an attack by Aceh. The composer himself may have been a Singaporean; this would account for the fact that the first sections glorify Singapore as the first great Malay trading port. The compiler took great pains to ensure the reader (or listener; the text may have been intended to be recited to audiences rather than read individually) of the veracity of the stories he set in Singapore. He frequently alludes to specific landmarks in Singapore that could be seen in his day as proof that what he wrote was true. This literary device does not occur in any other sections of the text.

We know that numerous ports in the Malay realm, from Kedah on the Malay Peninsula to Palembang in south Sumatra, were earlier Malay centres of long-distance trading spheres of interaction. The compiler of the *Raffles MS 18* does give Seguntang Hill in Palembang an important role as the place where the young man destined to become Singapore's founder first appeared and where he was recognized as a man destined for greatness, but he soon deserted Palembang with all his followers and went in search of a better place to found an exemplary centre.

Before the young prince makes his appearance, however, the link between his personal destiny and Singapore's fate is already foreshadowed when his father, a great conqueror from South India, meets emissaries sent to intercept him at Temasek. His father, Raja Chulan (a thinly disguised figure modelled on Rajaraja Chola, a real person who conquered Palembang and other prominent Malay ports in 1025), then explored the Singapore Strait and discovered an underwater kingdom there. He married the princess of that kingdom and had three sons, but he prefigured his son's later wandering spirit by becoming homesick for his homeland in India. He returns to the mouth of the Temasek (later Singapore) River on a winged horse, and had his artificers carve the record of his underwater exploration on a boulder there, under which he hid treasure for his three sons to find when they came of age.

The story of the foreign prince who marries an undersea princess is a trope found widely in Southeast Asia. Early Chinese sources record the story of the marriage of an Indian prince named Kambu and a *naga* (serpent divinity) queen, who become the progenitors of the rulers of Kambujadesa (Cambodia). A Chinese emissary, Zhou Daguan, heard the same story when he visited Angkor in 1296. The Javanese kingdoms of Surakarta and Yogyakarta trace their origins to a pact between Senapati and Loro Kidul, "Queen of the South", who lives beneath the Indian Ocean. The compiler of the *Malay Annals* was obviously familiar with this trope.

What More Would We Like to Know about the Malay Annals?

When did this story of the foreign prince first appear in the Singapore context? A lead statue found near the mouth of the Singapore River (at Empress Place) during archaeological research there in 1998[3] is unique in the art of Southeast Asia. In addition to its use of lead as a material for sculpture, it depicts a male figure riding a horse in a two-dimensional style highly reminiscent of the *wayang kulit* puppets that is also found on east Javanese stone murals of the thirteenth century temple Candi Jago. It is possible that this statue was made in Singapore during the fourteenth century, and was actually meant to depict Singapore's legendary founder.

Although the *Malay Annals* is not a reliable guide to the facts of Temasek's history, it provides a useful insight into the possible ways in which Singapore was perceived when the British arrived in 1819, and why Singapore grew as quickly as it did. Stamford Raffles believed that Singapore was a historic site and that it was well-known to the population of the region. We do not know on what information he based his conclusion, but it is likely that he discussed the subject with his Malay acquaintances, facilitated by his undoubted ability to speak, read and write Malay, a skill which few of his East India Company colleagues appear to have possessed.

Despite the importance of the *Malay Annals* for understanding the sociocultural matrix of the population of the southern Straits of Melaka and Riau, no critical edition of the variant texts has yet been compiled. This would entail comparing the different versions of the text, creating a genealogy for them, and a tentative reconstruction of the original or "core" text. This is one of the fields that one hopes will be developed in the future.

Chinese Sources

In the early twentieth century, a work written in 1349 entitled *Daoyi zhilue* was translated into English.[4] The author, Wang Dayuan, was the first merchant to describe Southeast Asia. He wrote about ninety-nine different places, three of which relate to Singapore. Wang described two ports in Temasek. One was located at *Longya men*, which was a strait "between the two hills of the *Danmaxi* barbarians" who were ruled by a *qiu zhang*, "tribal chief".[5] This phrase is used to refer to the leader of a tribe or society who rules through charisma and prowess.[6] They also had a *xiang fu* ("prime minister or high official") who *shou nan nui jian zong guo ren ju zi duo*, "instructed (in the sense of issuing a regulation) man woman both and in relation to each other Chinese people live more (suggesting harmony)".[7] This usually is glossed as meaning that an official instructed his subjects to live in harmony with the Chinese. It is possible that this referred to a Chinese community. Wang uses this phrase once more, in connection with a settlement of Chinese soldiers who had been set ashore on an island called Gou Lan Shan off the southwest coast of Borneo in 1292, and who were still there in the 1330s.[8] This is strong evidence in favour of the inference that Chinese were residing in Temasek.

The people of *Longya men* wore rather simple clothing and were said to wear their hair long, tied in a bun. The Chinese brought such goods as floral-patterned cloth, iron pans and ordinary ceramics (*chu ci qi*) to trade.

In the very next breath he says that the local population were pirates who stole Quanzhou products, who did not molest ships going west, but who would send fleets of 200 or 300 vessels to attack them on the return voyage to China. If the ships were overcome, the crews would be slaughtered. These seem almost like accounts of two different places. Perhaps Wang had two different experiences in *Longya men*; he is thought to have made two trading voyages to Southeast Asia.

In another section he discusses *Banzu*, which is "linked to the hill behind the *Longya men*", and thus also forms part of Temasek. People live on terraces around the hill. The inhabitants were quite distinct from the *Longya men* people. They wore their hair short and wore headgear of "false gold-patterned satin". They busied themselves with such occupations as salt production and brewing rice wine. They also had a chief. The inhabitants were characterized as honest traders with whom the Chinese exchanged red gold and ceramics.

Temasek (*Danma xi*) appears in another context, under the description of *Xian*, believed to refer to the lower Chao Phraya valley of Thailand. The *Xian*/Shan/Siamese were known to be expanding into the lower Malay Peninsula in the late thirteenth century. In Wang's account of *Xian*, he mentions that they had recently attacked Temasek with seventy junks, but the port was well defended and the siege failed.[9] The remnants of the "Old Malay Wall" were still visible on maps of Singapore drawn in 1819[10] and 1822.[11]

What More Would We Like to Know about the *Daoyi zhilue*?

First, there is still no complete English translation of Wang Dayuan's text. Even if there is no more information about Temasek to be gleaned from his text, we would like to know more about Wang himself. His own history is poorly known. The sections that Rockhill did not translate in 1914 might be able to shed some light on him. Second, new advances in Chinese philology might make it possible to improve on Rockhill's translation. Third, more is definitely known about the identifications of some of the places named in Wang's text. It would be useful to add new annotations to reflect these improvements.

The Singapore Stone

In 1819 a large boulder that had been artificially split in two was discovered at the rocky point at the mouth of the Singapore River. One face of the boulder bore writing in a script used in ancient Indonesia and the Malay Peninsula. Scholars disagree about the age of the script[12] and the nature of its contents. One fragment of the stone is now in the National Museum of Singapore. Two other fragments are believed to be in the India Museum in Kolkata, but efforts to locate them have not succeeded. It might be possible to discern more facts about the inscription if more pieces of it could be studied.

British Intelligence about the Singapore Region in December 1818

In June 1818 Colonel William Farquhar had already gone on a scouting voyage in the southern Straits and had obtained a favourable impression of Karimun Island. Karimun is now known to archaeologists and historians as the site of a tenth-century inscription written in Sanskrit language and Nagari script. In the fourteenth century it was a rendezvous for Chinese shipping on the way through the Dragon's Tooth Strait between Sentosa and Singapore Island.[13] The *Orang Laut* who brought Parameswara to Singapore in the fourteenth century lived at Karimun.[14] After Captain Alexander Hamilton visited Singapore in 1699, an anonymous cartographer charted the entrance to what is now Keppel Harbour in 1709.[15] It is not known whether Raffles was aware of this map, or what other sources of intelligence the British had about Singapore before Raffles's expedition arrived here in January 1819. It would be useful to know who made the map of 1709, and why.

Prehistoric Singapore

The prehistory of Singapore is another topic that has not been systematically investigated. Two areas in Singapore have yielded pebble tools typical of the Neolithic era in Southeast Asia. Some were found on Pulau Ubin; others were recovered from Tanjong Karang, a point of land just north of Tuas on Singapore's southwest coast. Neither of these have been excavated, though a team from the Raffles Museum under H.D. Collings did excavate a site called Tanjong Bunga on what is now the Malaysian side of the West Reach. The results of this excavation were never published, but a summary of them was compiled by Michael Tweedie based on notes in the museum's register.[16]

What Would We Like to Know about Prehistoric Singapore?

The short answer is, almost everything. No other information about pre-Temasek Singapore is available. Tanjong Karang would be a good place to begin, but unfortunately that area of Singapore is off-limits to the public.

In the Bags: Deciphering Discoveries from
Thirty-five Years of Systematic Excavations

The remains discovered in 1984 were sufficient to confirm that the *Danmaxi* mentioned by Wang Dayuan in 1349 was in fact Singapore. The excavations since that time have been aimed at elucidating the character of that port. No other fourteenth-century Southeast Asian port has been subjected to as much archaeological scrutiny as Singapore. In fact, no other fourteenth-century port in the region has yet been excavated. For comparison, one has to look at earlier or later

Figure 2.1 The 1984 Excavation at Fort Canning.

sites, which cannot be directly compared, since Singapore has a unique combination of historical and archaeological evidence for early overseas Chinese settlement.

The vast majority of the artefacts found are ceramics; about half were made locally, and half were imported from China. The local ceramics are typical of wares made in Peninsular Malaysia, Sumatra and Riau; they were probably made by the local Malay population. The Chinese wares include both high-quality porcelain and utilitarian stonewares. The porcelains were used by both elite and commoners, but some unique items found on Fort Canning were extremely rare and were probably used by the royalty.

Fort Canning Hill was definitely an area used by the upper class, but some craftsmen also worked there, making artefacts of gold and glass. The area between the Singapore River and the Malay Wall (now Stamford Road) was densely occupied by people who worked copper and iron and who probably engaged in many other activities connected with import-export trade.

What More Could We Learn about Singapore from Artefacts?

Database Project

The analysis of the artefacts has only reached a superficial, qualitative level. The sorting, counting and analysis of the artefacts is a long, slow process that requires trained experts. An online database project was launched in 2018 with support from the Singapore National Heritage Board (http://epress.nus.edu.sg/sitereports). The first database uploaded to this site contains data on approximately five thousand artefacts from an excavation conducted on the Padang.[17] More site reports have now been uploaded to the site, including databases on an excavation on the Dieng Plateau in Java, a system for classification of ceramics from Bagan, Myanmar, and a shipwreck site in Indonesia. More databases for other sites in Singapore, as well as comparative sites in Southeast Asia, are being compiled. The long-term goal of the project is to make Singapore a centre for dissemination of data on Southeast Asian historical archaeology, and to encourage multinational collaboration. At present it is very difficult to make detailed comparisons with other early historic cities in Southeast Asia. This project is meant to alleviate that problem.

Physical and Chemical Analysis

This type of research is necessary in order to trace the origins of imported items of ceramics, glass and metal and to understand the uses of various objects.

Environmental Studies

The white sand beach mentioned in the *Malay Annals* as the attribute that attracted Sri Tribuana to come to Temasek was discovered in the excavation at the Padang in 2003. Where did the white sand come from? It extends from the Padang to Kampung Gelam. The subject of coastal change and geomorphology of Singapore has not been seriously studied. Preliminary research at Bras Basah Park showed that the area had long been a swamp before humans arrived. So where did the white sand come from? The early vegetation of Singapore can also be explored by using such techniques as palynology and phytolith analysis. Studies of the geomorphology of Singapore's coasts will also be useful in determining the relationship between human activity and the maritime environment in pre-modern times.

Other Areas for Exploration

Underwater archaeology in Singapore theoretically holds great potential; at least one ancient shipwreck has been found, at Pulau Nipah on the Indonesian side of the Singapore Strait. Sentosa (Belakang Mati) is a candidate for a base for the pirates whom Wang Dayuan mentioned. Neolithic tools were found at Tuas in the 1890s and on Ubin in the 1930s. Thai Buddhist bronzes are said to have been found at Ponggol. Ming porcelains were dredged up in the Kallang basin. Pre-1819 earthenware sherds have been found on Pulau Tekong.

Figure 2.2 The white sand mentioned in the *Malay Annals* is visible in this excavation at Istana Kampung Gelam.

One other location where archaeological remains have purportedly been found is Ponggol. In the 1990s a hobbyist who used a metal detector to scour Singapore's beaches displayed a number of bronze items that he claimed he had found there. These objects, all heavily corroded, included a human face, possibly of Buddha; a disc-shaped object, possibly a parasol for a Buddha statue; and a human head with a pointed crown typical of Thai-style Buddhist imagery of the fifteenth-century Ayutthaya kingdom.

The potential importance of Singapore's northeast coast for archaeological research indicated by the stone tools from Pulau Ubin and these bronzes is further emphasized by the results of a brief survey conducted on western Pulau Tekong in 1987 as part of a larger ASEAN-supported research project. At the site of Kampong Permatang, potsherds exposed by a bulldozer during land levelling

Figure 2.3 Bronze head of an Ayutthaya-style Buddha.

included a small quantity of earthenware sherds decorated with carved paddle impressed designs and cord marking, and a glazed sherd identified as Sukhothai ware, which like the bronzes noted above was made in Thailand in the fifteenth century.[18] The northeast coast of Singapore including the Ponggol area and Pulau Tekong is strategic due to the fact that this coast is sheltered from the northeast monsoon and affords a position from which to monitor shipping entering the Johor River estuary or passing along Singapore's south coast towards the Dragon's Tooth Strait. In the early seventeenth century, Dutch ships and their Malay allies used this area to launch a surprise attack on Portuguese ships coming from Macao.

Further Questions

Were there any other ports in the Singapore region? Where are some of the other sites in the Singapore area mentioned by Wang Dayuan?

Preliminary research on Bintan and Batam has revealed that these islands were part of Singapore's sphere of trade in the fourteenth century. It would be very useful to know how Singapore related to its neighbours in Riau, Sumatra and Malaysia.

Figure 2.4 Excavations at Empress Place.

What were Singapore's links with other kingdoms in Southeast Asia? We have recovered fifteenth-century glazed stoneware from north-central Thailand and northern Vietnam in Singapore; can we find more evidence of such links? Some unusual earthenware from fourteenth-century Singapore may have come from Kalimantan or South Thailand, along with pottery known as Fine Paste Ware found here. Other sherds may have come from Myanmar.

The lives of ordinary Singaporeans of the nineteenth century are poorly documented by historical sources. Some excavations have been conducted at Duxton Hill and Istana Kampong Glam. Other sites in downtown Singapore have yielded artefacts of both phases of Singapore's history (the fourteenth–sixteenth and nineteenth–twentieth centuries). Archaeology has the potential to recover forgotten information about life on the island during the British colonial era. It would be interesting and informative to compare the standard of living and commerce in Singapore with other British colonies of that period, including those areas where Chinese immigrants were also living.

As this list of questions shows, even without further excavations, enough data connected with Singapore's past already exists to keep scholars occupied for years.

Notes

1. L.Y. Andaya, *The Kingdom of Johor 1641–1728: Economic and Political Developments* (Kuala Lumpur: Oxford University Press, 1975), pp. 256, 259, 264, 281, 288.

2. C.C. Brown, trans. and ed., *Sejarah Melayu or Malay Annals* (Kuala Lumpur: Oxford University Press, 1970).

3. J.N. Miksic, "Sebuah arca timah hitam dari Tebing Sungai Singapura [A lead statue recently discovered at a Majapahit-period site in Singapore]". Eighth Scientific Archaeology Conference, Yogyakarta (Indonesia), 15–18 February 1999, in *Kumpulan Makalah Pertemuan Ilmiah Arkeologi VIII* (Jakarta: Ikatan Ahli Arkeologi Indonesia), pp. 425–28; J.N. Miksic, *Singapore and the Silk Road of the Sea, 1300–1800* (Singapore: NUS Press, 2013), p. 353.

4. W.W. Rockhill, "Notes on the Relations and Trade of China with the Eastern Archipelago and the Coasts of the Indian Ocean during the Fourteenth Century", *T'oung Pao*, 2nd ser., 15 (1914): 419–47; 16 (1915): 61–159, 236–71, 374–92, 435–67, 604–26.

5. P. Wheatley, *The Golden Khersonese: Studies in the Historical Geography of the Malay Peninsula before A.D. 1500* (Kuala Lumpur: University of Malaya Press, 1961), p. 82; Hsu Yün-ts'iao, "Singapore in the Remote Past", *Journal of the Malaysian Branch of the Royal Asiatic Society* 45, no. 1 (1973): 2.

6. Personal Communication, Geoff Wade, 30 May 2010.

7. Ibid.

8. Rockhill, "Notes on the Relations and Trade of China", p. 26.

9. Ibid., p. 100.

10. Bute map in Miksic, *Singapore and the Silk Road of the Sea*, pp. x–xi.

11 Miksic, *Singapore and the Silk Road of the Sea*, p. 209; British Library IOR: X/3347.

12. Miksic, *Singapore and the Silk Road of the Sea*, pp. 13–16.

13. Wheatley, *Golden Khersonese*, p. 82.

14. A. Cortesao, trans. and ed., *The Suma Oriental of Tomé Pires: An Account of the East, from the Red Sea to Japan, written in Malacca and India in 1512–1515 and the Book of Francisco Rodrigues, Rutter of a Voyage in the Red Sea, Nautical Rules, Almanack and Maps, Written and Drawn in the East Before 1515*, 2 vols. Hakluyt Society, 2nd ser. vols. 39 and 40 (London: Hakluyt Society, 1944), p. 233.

15. British Library K38266; Miksic, *Singapore and the Silk Road of the Sea*, p. 145.

16. M.W.F. Tweedie, "The Stone Age in Malaya", *Journal of the Malayan Branch of the Royal Asiatic Society* 26, no. 2 (1953): 84–85.

17. J.N. Miksic, "Southeast Asian Archaeological Site Reports, Singapore No. 1: The Singapore Cricket Club Excavation", April 2003, https://doi.org/10.25717/7w0e-3n3c.

18. "Fourth Intra-ASEAN Archaeological and Conservation Workshop 1987", unpublished report, pp. 37–45.

3

Regional Influences, International Geopolitics and Environmental Factors in the Rise and Demise of Temasek

Derek Heng

Often, when we survey the indigenous sources on the founding of port-settlements and polities in the region of the Melaka Straits, we are given the impression that human agency was the prime factor that resulted in their rise and decline. While the important role of human agency cannot be denied, it is crucial for us to also consider the role of exogenous factors in creating the conditions necessary for the creation of the required geopolitical contexts for urban generation and the state formational process to occur. This is particularly so for small port-settlements and port politics in the Melaka Straits. What were the regional circumstances that allowed for localized autonomy to be viable and the opportunity for sufficient economic self-sustainability to be developed in these settlements, especially Temasek?

Exogenous forces were, however, not confined solely to political vicissitudes at the regional and international levels. Environmental events, the occurrences of which were often beyond the control of humans but which had an impact on human activities and historical trajectories, also affected the rise and demise of port-polities in the Melaka Straits region. What were the environmental factors of the first half of the second millennium CE that affected the fortunes of Temasek?

Finally, given the role of macro-level forces and environmental factors in the fortunes of port-settlements and polities in the Straits region, it is not difficult to expect that these exogenous factors would have played a part in generating the identity and culture of the port-polities in question. What, then, were the external influences on Temasek's culture and identity?

The present essay seeks to discuss the above three issues and the role they played in the formation, establishment and demise of Temasek during the late thirteenth century through to the early fifteenth century.

Regional Forces in Maritime Asia and the Rise of Temasek

While port settlements of the Melaka Straits region were externally oriented, their respective locations determined to a large extent the direction of that orientation. Settlements in the north Melaka Straits region, for example, were generally oriented towards the Bay of Bengal and the Indian subcontinent. Conversely, settlements located in the south Straits region tended to be oriented towards the Java Sea and South China Sea. Consequently, development in these respective littoral zones in Maritime Asia had a direct impact on the state-formational processes and developments in the Melaka Straits region.

As an example, Śrīvijaya's rise as a regional thalassocracy in the seventh century was enabled by China's passive stance towards maritime trade from across the South China Sea during the Tang dynasty.[1] This posture, of being interested in maritime trade while not allowing Chinese merchants to sail to Southeast Asia and beyond to engage in trade, led to the creation of opportunities for Śrīvijaya to fill the vacuum and to bring to China the foreign commodities it wanted.[2]

The result was that Śrīvijaya managed to establish its regional authority over the Melaka Straits region, up to South Kedah and the Isthmus of Kra, from the seventh through the twelfth centuries.[3] For the Melaka Straits region, access to Chinese commodities and manufactures had to be obtained through Śrīvijaya. Importantly, economic and political autonomy was not possible under these international conditions and the regional structure that Śrīvijaya established.[4]

Localized political and economic autonomy in the Melaka Straits region was not possible when a strong regional power was in place. Apart from descriptions of landfall sites on the Isthmus of Kra and the north Malay Peninsula, there is no textual record of autonomous polities in the Melaka Straits region during the late first millennium CE. It was only in the early tenth century that a semblance of autonomy began to appear in the north Melaka Straits region. An ascendant and proactive Chola

Kingdom, dominating the Coromandel Coast, had begun to extend its commercial networks and naval capabilities across the Bay of Bengal into the north Melaka Straits. This created a countervailing condition against Śrīvijaya's regional hegemony and provided the opportunity for the ruler at the South Kedah settlement to exercise some measure of political autonomy. A number of polities along the Isthmus of Kra soon followed suit after that through to the thirteenth century.[5]

For the south Melaka Straits region, local autonomy for port-settlements came about in the late eleventh century. In 1090, China, under the Song court, liberated its maritime shipping regulations, permitting Chinese ships to sail to Southeast Asia for trade. Śrīvijaya's advantage vis-à-vis the China market, which it had enjoyed since the seventh century, was lost.[6] The regional hegemony it had established, which first began to break apart in the north Melaka Straits region in the tenth century, also began to disintegrate.

By the late twelfth century, Śrīvijaya had been reduced to being third in importance in China's trade with Southeast Asia. By 1225, the

Figure 3.1 Coarse stoneware bottles like these, with very small mouths, have been found in large quantities in excavations on and around Fort Canning Hill. These small-mouthed bottles would have been used to transport liquids, including sauces and liquor. These two bottles were found by fishermen in their nets somewhere in the Riau islands and they ended up on the back shelf of an antiques dealer in Singapore. (Photo by C.G. Kwa.)

number of ports that were known to the Chinese as being open for trade had increased, with a number of these ports in the north Melaka Straits region being politically autonomous.[7] By the early fourteenth century, the number of autonomous port-settlements in the region had increased to over twenty.[8] It was during this time that Temasek was established at the end of the thirteenth century.

Environmental Factors

These broader changes in trans-regional geopolitics in Maritime Asia did not develop on their own. Environmental forces also played a role in changing the natural environment, both in the littoral regions of Maritime Asia as well as on Continental Asia, upon which the geopolitical structures of the late first and early second millennia were built. This change in the natural environment disrupted the economic and political systems across Asia and Europe and created a different environment upon which a different group of polities could proliferate through the thirteenth and fourteenth centuries.

To begin with, the late twelfth and early thirteenth centuries saw the end of a centuries-long medieval warming period and the start of a prolonged period of atmospheric cooling. This prolonged cooling led to several natural phenomena. Firstly, the decreasing temperatures across continental Asia in summer resulted in a narrower oscillation of the inter-tropical convergence zone, a band of rainclouds that oscillates north and south of the solar equator. This narrower oscillation meant that tropical rainfall was no longer reaching the latitudes, both in the north and south, as it had previously.[9] The reduction in summer rainfall, coupled with overall decreases in temperature, consequently led to an overall decrease in agricultural output across the tropical and sub-tropical zones from the thirteenth century onwards.[10]

The cooling across Europe and Continental Asia also resulted in a reduction in terrestrial temperatures. The result was that the range of arable land, both in Europe and Asia, decreased dramatically. Areas that were previously arable during the medieval warming period, such as higher-altitude zones in Europe, were no longer arable because of the fall in overall land temperatures. Additionally, the growing seasons of other arable land became increasingly shorter during the period of lowering land temperatures.[11]

For tropical Southeast Asia, the reduction in rainfall from the narrower oscillation of the inter-tropical convergence zone was further exacerbated by the increase in incidence of the El Niño effect in the Pacific Ocean. This led to a reduction in the occurrences of year-end rains that would otherwise have come in from the Pacific Ocean.[12]

All of these environmental changes, which led to consistent periods of prolonged drought in summer and winter in Asia and wetter and colder summers in Europe, resulted in an overall collapse of agricultural output across Asia and Europe through the course of the thirteenth and fourteenth centuries.[13] It is important to note the collapse of tier-one states across these two continents, including the Abbasid Caliphate, Song China, the Chola Kingdom and Byzantine Rome.

It may not be an interesting coincidence that Temasek, along with a plethora of small port-settlements and polities in the Melaka Straits region, was established through the course of the turbulent thirteenth and fourteenth centuries.

Local Autonomy and Being Caught in Between

Southeast Asia of the late thirteenth and the fourteenth century, during which period Temasek was active, was not devoid of regional powers. Even as Śrīvijaya, the hitherto regional hegemonic state of the Melaka Straits region, had come to an end by 1275, in the west Java Sea region, Majapahit in Java was on an ascendency. In the Gulf of Siam, the key regional power was Sukhothai in the early fourteenth century, followed by the more powerful Ayutthaya in the second half of the fourteenth century onwards. These regional powers sought to keep the various port settlements and polities within their respective spheres of authority, even as these settlements and polities were able to operate autonomously. Clearly, autonomy did not mean necessarily the absence of a regional hegemonic power, but how those regional powers viewed and exerted their regional influence.

There were three primary means by which imperialism and regional influence could be exerted. The first was territorial control and administration, in which territories and communities were brought under direct administration of a regional power. This required the deployment of coercive force to keep the imperial structure intact. The second was through economic co-dependency, in which asymmetrical economic relationships were established, tying a lower centre and its population to a higher central economic core.[14] The third was through cultural imperialism, or soft power, in which a regional power would exert influence and recognition of its superiority over smaller centres and populations by imposing cultural adaptation, assimilation and articulation of key cultural traits from the former on to the latter.

In the case of Temasek, while the polity was autonomous and never territorially or administratively controlled by Majapahit, Sukhothai or Ayutthaya, it was nonetheless overshadowed by the economic and cultural influences of these powers.

Javanese influence over Temasek was apparent from textual records and archaeology. Textually, both indigenous records, such as the

Sulalatus-Salatin, and those from further afield, including Javanese texts such as the *Desawarnana/Nāgarakṛtāgama* and *Pararaton,* and Chinese texts such as the *Daoyi zhilue,* note that Majapahit exerted significant pressure, both militarily and economic, over Temasek. This has also been borne out in the archaeological data recovered from Temasek-period sites in Singapore. Decorative arts and jewellery, high language, as well as such permanent writings as the Singapore Stone, illustrate the influence of Javanese high culture in Temasek.[15]

The influence of Javanese political culture also appeared to have influenced the notion of the characteristics of an ideal polity. The navy, as a state entity needed to engender trade, would establish a polity's sphere of influence and the creation of a cosmopolitan urban centre. As a socio-political ideal based on Majapahit as the model, the navy was regarded as an indispensable arm that provided the state with the necessary coercive force to engender stature and success. The size of the navy, and the prowess of its commanders, became the means of establishing a polity's status vis-à-vis other polities in the Melaka Straits region.[16]

Economically, the presence of Javanese picis and Chinese copper cash, both of which were used as coinage in the Javanese economy in the late thirteenth and the fourteenth century, suggest that Java was an important trading partner of Temasek.

Temasek was also influenced from across the Gulf of Siam. Tai influence, compared to Javanese influence, was a little more understated, but nonetheless just as important. This influence could be discerned from the hydrological systems that were constructed in Temasek, including the moat that ran from the catchment areas at the foot of Mount Sophia and Fort Canning to the sea, which was likely used for agricultural purposes, and the soil retention earth rampart that ran on the south side of that moat and around the western foot of Fort Canning Hill.[17] Both types of features have been utilized in Gulf of Siam littoral, including at such sites as Khao Sam Kheo, Satingpra and U Thong, to name but a few.[18]

Decline of Temasek and the Role of International and Regional Exigencies

Temasek, as an autonomous polity, lasted for only a little over a century. By the early fifteenth century, a new port-polity had emerged at Melaka, and Temasek receded in importance thereafter. The decline of Temasek has hitherto been explained as the outcome of the rise of Melaka.[19] This is, of course, not necessarily inaccurate. Melaka's rise in the fifteenth century was based on its ability to capitalize on changes in China's approach to international geopolitics and foreign relations with

Southeast Asia under the Ming Dynasty. The Ming imperial voyages of Zheng He, under the patronage of the Ming Emperor Yongle (r. 1402–24), leading to the recognition of Melaka as a vassal state by the Ming court, enabled the assuaging of Tai expansionism in the Malay Peninsula through a treaty of protection both with the Ming court and Ayutthaya.[20] In this regard, the shift in regional geopolitical outlook, particularly of the Chinese state, resulted in a cascade of effects in the Melaka Straits region and Gulf of Siam littoral that led to the eclipse of a nascent polity over other pre-existing ones, including Temasek.[21]

According to Portuguese accounts written in the sixteenth century, after Melaka signed an agreement with Ayutthaya, agreeing to pay the latter an annual sum in exchange for control over Temasek, the economy of Temasek gradually began to be hollowed out as merchants began to relocate to Melaka.[22] The *Sulalatus-Salatin* notes that the move of the kingdom of Singapura from Temasek to Melaka was spurred by a *successful* attack that was launched by Majapahit forces.[23] Both accounts indicate that the geopolitical arrangements in the Melaka Straits region had changed dramatically from the early fifteenth century on, swinging back towards regional hegemony and away from localized autonomy.

However, the historical accounts also allude to the possibility of environmental factors that may have led to the decline of Temasek as a port, and as a result of that decline, the demise of the polity as well. Portuguese accounts, for example, have noted that the waters around Singapore were not conducive for ships to anchor off the southern shores of the island. Apparently, there were strong storms that would break out in that area during the time that ships would typically be sheltering in the waters around the western entrance to Keppel Harbour waiting for the tide to change and carry them through the narrow entrance into the harbour. That would have been between September and January, based on the continental monsoon patterns. This period of the year, coinciding with the trade winds generated by the inter-tropical convergence zone, suggests that the global cooling trend, evident from the thirteenth century onwards, had continued through the fifteenth and sixteenth centuries, leading to a higher level of storm activities accompanying the lingering of the convergence zone along the equatorial zone for prolonged periods annually.

Another regional environmental factor, particularly during the late fourteenth and the fifteenth century, also has to be considered. Studies of the swale stratigraphy of coastal caves along the northwest coast of Sumatra have indicated that the northern Melaka Straits region experienced at least two major seismic events off the northwest coast of Sumatra, which resulted in tsunamis affecting the north coast of Sumatra—around 1394, and around 1450. The 1394 event resulted in the devastation of coastal settlements along the north coast of Sumatra, as well as the west coast of the Isthmus of Kra, while the 1450 event likely reinforced the devastation. The result, based on ceramic finds, suggest that the settlements that had developed along the north Melaka Straits coastline were wiped out, and new settlements did not regenerate and grow until the end of the fifteenth century onwards.[24]

These environmental events likely provided the vacuum, at least in the north Melaka Straits, for nascent port-settlements, such as Melaka, to capitalize upon, to build a regional hegemonic structure in the Melaka Straits. Additionally, ports such as Melaka were able to grow their trade across the Bay of Bengal to its geopolitical advantage. It is likely not a coincidence that one of the largest communities of foreign traders at Melaka in the fifteenth century were the Gujaratis.[25] For port polities such as Temasek, the rise of a regional power in the Melaka Straits signalled the reversion to a structure that saw port settlements in the region subsumed under a thalassocratic system.

Concluding Thoughts: Temasek, the International World and the Environment

This narrative suggests that for port settlements and port polities of the Melaka Straits region and Malay region, regional and international circumstances played a substantial role in state-formational processes and the ability of settlements to be able to express local political autonomy in the pre-modern era. Specifically, in the case of Temasek, trans-regional and international vicissitudes led to the set of conditions that brought the demise of seven centuries of regional hegemony in the Melaka Straits region and opened up the necessary conditions for economic and political autonomy.

In this regard we should bear in mind that the absence of local autonomy, lasting for six centuries from the inception of Śrīvijaya in the seventh century to the early thirteenth century, recurred in the fifteenth century with the advent of Melaka. Conversely, the mushrooming of autonomous settlements occurred only in the thirteenth and fourteenth centuries. The fact that it took only a few decades for autonomous settlements to arise in the Melaka Straits region suggests that the social organization and state-formation processes of the riparian societies in the Straits region were easily disposed towards localized autonomy. In that regard, socio-political organization in the region was, at the lowest level, the port-settlement. However, developments in the Melaka Straits had a tendency towards regional hierarchical systems.

Even as port-settlements and polities were able to exercise local autonomy in the thirteenth and fourteenth centuries, regional influences, and the need to articulate regional cultural traits, appear to have been real imperatives for these settlements and polities. These influences were either assimilated and localized, or articulated for external consumption.

Finally, the role that environmental factors played in state-formational processes in the Melaka Straits have to be given due consideration. Such factors, including such global and long-term trends as global cooling, changes to the oscillation of the inter-tropical convergence zone and higher frequencies of occurrences of El Niño in the Pacific Ocean, led to changes in rainfall patterns and even storm patterns in maritime and continental Asia. These changes in turn impacted both the agricultural output of land-based societies and the navigational challenges faced by maritime societies. Added to these global environmental factors are regional events, including seismic activities, which had a direct impact on state-formational and regional geopolitics. Even as Temasek was a localized polity, its rise, activity and demise were intimately tied to international and regional developments. In this regard, Temasek's history needs to be understood through a global and regional lens.

Notes

1. Wang Gungwu, *The Nanhai Trade: The Early History of Chinese Trade in the South China Sea* (1958; repr., Singapore: Times Academic Press, 1998), pp. 69–110; Jitsuzô Kuwabara, *P'u Shou-Kêng, A Man of the Western Regions, Who Was the Superintendent of the Trading Ships' Office in Ch'üan-chou, Towards the End of the Sung Dynasty,* Memoirs of the Research Department no. 7 (Tokyo: The Toyo Bunko, 1935).

2. O.W. Wolters, *Early Indonesian Commerce: A Study of the Origins of Śrīvijaya* (1967: repr., New York, NY: American Council of Learned Societies, 2010); Derek Heng, *Sino-Malay Trade and Diplomacy from the Tenth through the Fourteenth Century* (Singapore: Institute of Southeast Asian Studies, 2012).

3. George Coedès, "Collected Studies", in *Sriwijaya: History, Religion & Language of an Early Malay Polity: Collected Studies,* edited by P.-Y. Manguin and M. Sheppard (Kuala Lumpur: Malaysian Branch of the Royal Asiatic Society, 1992); H. Kulke, "Śrīvijaya Revisited: Reflections on State Formation of a Southeast Asian Thalassocracy", *Bulletin De L'École Française D'Extrême-Orient* 102 (2016): 45–95; Michel Jacq-Hergoualc'h, *The Malay Peninsula: Crossroads of the Maritime Silk Road (100 BC – 1300 AD),* translated by Victoria Hobson, in *Handbuch der Orientalistik,* section 3, "Southeast Asia", vol. 13 (Leiden: Brill, 2002).

4. Hermann Kulke, "'Kadātuan Śrīvijaya'—Empire or Kraton of Śrīvijaya? A Reassessment of the Epigraphical Evidence", *Bulletin De L'École Française D'Extrême-Orient* 80, no. 1 (1993): 159–180; Kenneth R. Hall, *A History of Early Southeast Asia: Maritime Trade and Societal Development, 100–1500* (Lanham, MD: Rowman & Littlefield, 2011), pp. 103–34.

5. Derek Heng, "Situating Temasik within the Larger Regional Context: Maritime Asia and Malay State Formation in the Pre-modern Era". In Derek Heng and Syed Muhd Khairudin Aljunied, eds., *Singapore in Global History* (Amsterdam: Amsterdam University Press, 2011), pp. 32–33.

6. Heng, *Sino Malay Trade*, pp. 48–49; Derek Heng, "Structures, Networks and Commercial Practices of Private Chinese Maritime Traders in Island Southeast Asia in the Early Second Millennium AD", *International Journal of Maritime History* 20, no. 2 (2008): 27–54.

7. For a detailed account of the autonomous port settlements that were emerging in the early thirteenth century, refer to Friedrich Hirth and William Woodville Rockhill, *Chau Ju-Kua: His Work on the Chinese and Arab Trade in the Twelfth and Thirteenth Centuries, Entitled Chu-fanchï* (1911; repr., New York: Paragon Book Reprint Corp., 1966).

8. For a detailed account of the autonomous port settlements that were emerging in the fourteenth century, refer to Su Jiqing, *Daoyi zhilue jiaoshi* (Beijing: Zhonghua shu ju, 2000).

9. Roger Graham Barry and Richard J. Chorley, *Atmosphere, Weather and Climate* (London: Routledge, 2010), pp. 225–26; G. Yancheva, N. Nowaczyk, J. Mingram et al., "Influence of the Intertropical Convergence Zone on the East Asian Monsoon", *Nature* 445 (2007): 74–77.

10. N. Pumijumnong, "Dendrochronology in Southeast Asia", *Trees* 27 (2013): 343–58; W. Qian, Q. Hu, Y. Zhu et al., "Centennial-Scale Dry-Wet Variations in East Asia", *Climate Dynamics* 21 (2003): 77–89.

11. William Chester Jordan, *The Great Famine: Northern Europe in the Early Fourteenth Century* (Princeton, NJ: Princeton University Press, 1998).

12. K. Cobb, C. Charles, H. Cheng et al., "El Niño/Southern Oscillation and Tropical Pacific Climate during the Last Millennium", *Nature* 424 (2003): 271–76; Ashish Sinha, Stott Lowell, Max Berkelhammer et al., "A Global Context for Megadroughts in Monsoon Asia during the Past Millennium", *Quaternary Science Reviews* 30, nos. 1–2 (2011): 47–62.

13. C. Pfister, G. Schwarz-Zanetti, and M. Wegmann, "Winter Severity in Europe: The Fourteenth Century", *Climatic Change* 34 (1996): 91–108.

14. J. Burbank and F. Cooper, *Empires in World History: Power and the Politics of Difference* (Princeton, NJ, Princeton University Press, 2010), pp. 4–9; Derek Heng, "Trans-Regionalism and Economic Co-dependency in the South China Sea: The Case of China and the Malay Region (tenth to fourteenth centuries AD)", *International History Review* 35, no. 3 (2013): 486–510.

15. R.O. Winstedt, "Gold Ornaments Dug Up at Fort Canning, Singapore", *Journal of the Malayan Branch of the Royal Asiatic Society* 6, no. 4 (1928): 1–4; James Low, "An Account of Several Inscriptions Found in Province Wellesley on the Peninsula of Malacca", *Journal of the Asiatic Society of Bengal* 17, no. 2 (1848): 62–66.

16. Derek Heng, "State Formation and the Evolution of Naval Strategies in the Melaka Straits, c.500–1500 CE", *Journal of Southeast Asian Studies* 44, no. 3 (2013): 380–99.

17. Kwa Chong Guan, Derek Heng, Peter Borschberg, and Tan Tai Yong, *Seven Hundred Years: A History of Singapore* (Singapore: National Library Board/Marshall Cavendish, 2019), pp. 38–42.

18. Berenice Bellina et al., "The Early Development of Coastal Polities in the Upper Thai-Malay Peninsula", in *Before Siam: Essays in Art and Archaeology*, edited by Nicolas Revire and Stephen A. Murphy (Bangkok: River Books, 2014), pp. 68–89; Janice Stargardt, *Satingpra: The Environmental and Economic Archaeology of South Thailand*, British Archaeological Reports, Studies in Southeast Asian Archaeology no. 1 (Oxford: B.A.R., 1983); Paul Wheatley, *Negara and Commandry: Origins of the Southeast Asian Urban Traditions*, Research Papers nos. 207–8 (Chicago: University of Chicago Department of Geography, 1983), pp. 199–230.

19. Kwa Chong Guan, "From Temasik to Singapore: Locating a Global City-State in the Cycles of Melaka Straits History". In *Studying Singapore before 1800*, edited by Kwa Chong Guan and Peter Borschberg (Singapore: NUS Press, 2018), pp. 179–206.

20. B.W. Andaya and L.Y. Andaya, *A History of Malaysia*, 3rd ed. (New York: Palgrave Macmillan, 2017).

21. Andaya and Andaya, *History of Malaysia*, pp. 41–44.

22. Heng, "Situating Temasik", p. 48; Armando Cortesao, *The Suma Oriental of Tomé Pires: An Account of the East, from the Red Sea to Japan, Written in Malacca and India in 1512–1515. The Book of Francisco Rodrigues, Rutter of a Voyage in the Red Sea, Nautical Rules, Almanack and Maps, Written and Drawn in the East before 1515* (London: Hakluyt Society, 1944), p. 264.

23. C. C. Brown, *Sejarah Melayu or Malay Annals* (1953; repr., Kuala Lumpur: Oxford University Press, 1970), p. 50.

24. Patrick Daly, Kerry Sieh, Tai Yew Seng et al., "Archaeological Evidence That a Late 14th-century Tsunami Devastated the Coast of Northern Sumatra and Redirected History", *Proceedings of the National Academy of Sciences of the United States of America* 116, no. 24 (2019): 11679–11686, https://hdl.handle.net/10356/137353; K. Sieh, P. Daly, E.E. McKinnon et al., "Penultimate Predecessors of the 2004 Indian Ocean Tsunami in Aceh, Sumatra: Stratigraphic, Archeological, and Historical Evidence", *Journal of Geophysical Research: Solid Earth* 120, no. 1 (2015): 308–25, https://hdl.handle.net/10356/79433.

25. Andaya and Andaya, *A History of Malaysia*, p. 45.

4

The Mysterious Malay *Jong* and Other Temasek Shipping

Michael Flecker

With no reported shipwrecks in Singapore waters, we must draw on archaeological evidence from surrounding seas along with historical sources to investigate the wide range of ships that once called here. Apart from the European square riggers, it turns out that the eclectic mix of vessels anchored off the Singapore River during Raffles's early years, as depicted in paintings held in the National Museum (fig. 4.1), would not have differed much from the shipping of five centuries earlier. While numbers and makeup fluctuated with Singapore's changing status and with developments far afield, the diversity of shipping would have been maintained beyond fourteenth-century Temasek to at least the end of the seventeenth century.

Perhaps the earliest relevant archaeological discovery within this defined pre-colonial period is the *Nipa Shoal Wreck*. Nipa Shoal lies less than ten kilometres to the west of Raffles Lighthouse, within Indonesian territorial waters. The original finder, Warren Blake, donated most of the recovered artefacts to the National Museum. They include Longquan celadon dishes, stoneware jars and thousands of Chinese copper coins, the most recent providing an earliest possible wrecking date of 1258. The oldest coin dates to 762, illustrating the remarkable longevity of Chinese coin utilization, and implying that the actual wrecking date could be decades after 1258; the Longquan celedon suggests the late thirteenth century or beyond. Unfortunately, no hull remains were found. It is impossible to determine whether this ship had traded at the fledgling Temasek port before running afoul of the rocks as she journeyed further west. If she did, it is perhaps more likely that she was a Southeast Asian ship involved in the entrepôt trade. If she did not, she could have been a Chinese junk transiting the Singapore Strait during the northeast monsoon.

The *Jade Dragon Wreck* sank around the same time as the *Nipa Shoal Wreck* and with the same type of cargo, but off the northernmost tip of Borneo.[1] Unfortunately, the site was looted before archaeological intervention; however, hull remains confirm that the ship was of the Southeast Asian lashed-lug tradition. Planks were carved to shape and incorporated perforated lugs to which frames were lashed with *ijok* (sugar palm fibre). They were edge-joined with wooden dowels, which prior to the tenth century were augmented with internal stitches. Several bipod or tripod masts supported canted lug sails, and steering was by means of two quarter rudders. The well-known ninth-century Candi Borobudur ship carving is of this type, although the clearly depicted outriggers were probably not a feature of ocean-going merchant ships.

Figure 4.1 "View of Singapore from the Sea", with off-lying junks and a Southeast Asian vessel, *c*.1848. (Courtesy of the National Museum of Singapore, National Heritage Board.)

Figure 4.2 Planks with lugs and an overlying frame on the early 12th century Southeast Asian lashed-lug *Flying Fish Wreck*. (Flecker.)

The lashed-lug tradition lasted for well over a millennium, with the earliest archaeological encounter being the third-to-fifth-century CE Pontian ship in West Malaysia.[2]

The *Jade Dragon Wreck* is the youngest of a series of lashed-lug wrecks that have been found in Southeast Asian waters. Others include the mid-thirteenth-century *Java Sea Wreck* with a cargo of Fujian ceramics and iron,[3] the early-twelfth-century *Flying Fish Wreck* (fig. 4.2) with a similar but smaller cargo,[4] the early-twelfth-century *Lingga Wreck* with a cargo of Guangdong ceramics and iron,[5] the tenth-century *Cirebon Wreck* with an extremely diverse cargo loaded at an entrepôt such as Palembang,[6] and the tenth-century *Intan Wreck*, her little sister.[7]

It is highly likely that Southeast Asian lashed-lug craft called at Temasek. Interestingly, Temasek's fourteenth-century zenith coincided with the transition from lashed-lug assembly to fully dowelled construction. In the latter, planks were sawn rather than carved—a far less wasteful technique. They were fastened to frames with wooden dowels, or treenails. Dowel edge-joining was retained, and the external appearance is unlikely to have changed much. This new vessel type is referred to as a *jong*, an old Javanese term for ship.

By the time the Portuguese arrived in the early sixteenth century, *jongs*, or *juncos* as they called them, had achieved very large proportions.

From the description below, the encountered *jong* towered over the Portuguese flagship:

> Seeing that the junco wanted to start fighting, the Governor got close to her with his whole fleet. The galleys started shooting at her, but this did not affect her in the least, and she went on sailing.... The Portuguese ships then shot at her masts,... and she dropped her sails. Because she was very tall..., our people did not dare board her and our firing did not hurt her at all, for she had four superimposed layers of planks.... Seeing this, the Governor ordered his own *nau* to come alongside her. This was the *Flor de la Mar*, which had the highest castles of all. When she managed to board the junco, her aft castle barely reached her bridge.... [After two days and nights of fighting] the Governor decided to have the two rudders she carried outside torn away... [The junco then surrendered.][8] (Portuguese chronicler Gaspar Correia, describing an encounter in 1511).

Another Portuguese observation towards the end of the sixteenth century provides the best evidence for the construction of a *jong*. There is no comment on the attachment of the planks to the frames, which is sufficient to discount lashed-lug construction as that would have been quite an aberration for the Portuguese. Treenail joinery, on the other hand, was common in European ship construction. The absence of iron precludes nails or spikes. The mention of three rudders is probably erroneous. There would have been two quarter-rudders; however, perhaps the observed axial rudder was actually a substantial sternpost.

> In the whole of Java the common ships are the juncos; some of them are very big, like the very large *naos*. They are not nailed together, but are [built] with wooden dowels inserted into the seams of the planks, so that they are not seen from the outside; for when the planks are assembled, they are perforated with an auger and these dowels are inserted, which remain inside the fastened planks. They have two masts in addition to the mizzen mast.... [The sails] are made of woven rattan.... They have three rudders, one on each side and one in the middle.... There is nothing made of iron aboard these juncos.[9] (Father Nicolau Perreira S.J., 1582)

Interestingly, when the Dutch arrived only a couple of decades later, they observed Southeast Asian shipping of only modest size. Historian and archaeologist Pierre-Yves Manguin notes that the decline in vessel stature started much earlier, through instability caused by naval conflict and with the rise of competing Chinese and Gujarati long-distance trading fleets.[10] As an outpost of the Melaka Sultanate during the fifteenth century, a scaled-down Singapore would have played host to the largest of *jongs*. Small oared craft no doubt transferred cargo between these *jongs* and the sheltered banks of the Singapore River, in the manner of bumboats in more recent times. Under the Johor Shabandar (Harbour

Figure 4.3 A fine illustration of a *jong* with Southeast Asian canted lug sails (right), and another version with a battened square sail (left) in G.M.A.W. Lodewijcksz, *Premier livre de l'histoire de la navigation aux Indes Orientales, par les Hollandais*, Amsterdam, 1598.

Master) from the late sixteenth century, a resurgent Singapore would have received frequent visits from smaller *jongs*, partaking more in the peddling trade. Some would have sported the original Malay-style canted lug sails, while others would be rigged with fully battened square sails, perhaps reflecting Chinese hybridization. Both types are depicted side by side in early Dutch illustrations, confirming their coexistence (fig. 4.3).

Long-distance traders, indeed the longest-distance traders of the fourteenth century, were the Arabs and Persians who voyaged to and from China. Together with the Indians, they sailed in dhows that changed little in form and construction technique from the time of the Prophet. As a result of this continuity, we can turn to the only archaeological discoveries of Arab ships, the circa 826 CE *Belitung Wreck*[11] and the mid-ninth-century *Phanom Surin Wreck*,[12] for a picture of dhows trading with Temasek. Both ships were fully stitched with coir, inside the hull and out, with wadding keeping the plank joints sealed. A light section keel was augmented by a larger internal keelson and stringers. Frames were fastened to planks with coir or *ijok*. The stem was raked, while the stern was vertical. Quarter rudders were probably utilized during the ninth century; however, they were replaced with an axial rudder a century or two later. Stayed masts supported square sails, the triangular lateen rig only being adopted around the fifteenth century. The replica dhow, the *Jewel of Muscat*, on permanent display in the Resorts World Maritime Experiential Museum, is based on the *Belitung Wreck* remains and provides an authentic depiction of a ninth-century Arab or Indian dhow.

Apart from Southeast Asian earthenware, the majority of fourteenth-century finds from terrestrial excavations in Singapore consist of Chinese ceramics, the finer wares comprising *qingbai*, *shufu* and blue-and-white porcelain from Jingdezhen along with Longquan celadon from Zhejiang.[13] Prior to the twelfth century, most Chinese ceramic cargoes were transported on Southeast Asian ships. From the Southern Song dynasty (1127–1279), Chinese junks played a more significant role, although they were periodically banned from trading by the emperor of the day. The *Nanhai No. 1 Wreck* is a magnificent example of a massive Chinese junk bearing a full cargo of ceramics and iron for the Southeast Asian market.[14] She sank off Guangdong around 1183, making her one of the oldest oceanic Chinese junks so far discovered. By the fourteenth century, Chinese junks would have been a common sight off Temasek. As with the Arabs and Indians, Chinese shipwrights were very conservative, maintaining designs and construction methods for many centuries. Therefore, paintings of junks anchored in Singapore soon after the arrival of Raffles also provide a fine rendition of the junks that once traded with Temasek.

The *Binh Chau Wreck* is contemporaneous with the Temasek period. A smattering of Yuan blue-and-white porcelain in her cargo suggests a broad mid-fourteenth-century date. She was found in shallow water off central Vietnam carrying a Chinese ceramic cargo typical of that traded in Temasek, including brown-glazed stoneware and Longquan green-ware.[15] Perhaps she was destined for Temasek but foundered in a storm off a Vietnamese port while undertaking intermediate trade. She is a typical Chinese junk, fully iron-fastened, with a bluff bow, twelve bulkheads, tabernacle mast-supports and an axial rudder. Junks from southern China tended to have sea-friendly V-shaped hulls, whereas those from the north were more likely to be flat-bottomed for riverine and coastal trading.

One of the only junk losses contemporaneous with Zheng He's early fifteenth-century voyages is the *Bakau Wreck*.[16] She was lost off a small island to the east of Belitung in Indonesia while carrying a diverse ceramics cargo from China, Thailand and Vietnam. Interestingly, she was flat-bottomed, perhaps implying that ships from northern China were being called upon to supplement Zheng He's fleets or to fill the dearth they created. Such ships tend to perform poorly when not sailing downwind; however, innovations such as lee-boards could reduce leeway and thereby render them more viable.

Seventeenth-century Singapore is very poorly represented by archaeological finds. In fact, the only ceramics from this period were dredged up from the Kallang Basin during preparatory works for the Benjamin Sheares Bridge. They are products of Jingdezhen; however, decorations, including a trio of birds in flight, were copied by contemporaneous kilns elsewhere to capitalize on Jingdezhen's fame. The Zhangzhou kilns produced a relatively coarse ware incorporating many of Jingdezhen's designs and succeeded in winning over Japanese and Southeast Asian markets. A shipwreck with an almost exclusive cargo of Zhangzhou ceramics was discovered off Vietnam. The *Binh Thuan Wreck*[17] is another Chinese junk, which may have been positively identified through Dutch archives, a very rare circumstance (fig. 4.4). It would seem to be the ship of Captain I Sin Ho, which sank off Cambodia in 1608 with a cargo of "silk and other Chinese goods". In the seventeenth century, sea charts depict all of southern Vietnam as Cambodia. Most significantly, this ship is recorded as being bound for Johor. Therefore, Johor's Shabandaria, located on Singapore's central southern coast, may well have been the intended first stop.

Figure 4.4 Large Zhangzhou blue-and-white dishes on the *c.*1608 *Binh Thuan Wreck*. She was probably bound for Singapore. (Flecker.)

Thai ceramics from Si Satchanalai and Sukhothai have also been found in Singapore, albeit in small quantities. These Thai kilns ramped up production from the late fourteenth century through to the late sixteenth century in response to Chinese bans on overseas trade. The ships that transported most of the Thai ceramics were of Thai construction, although their design and construction were heavily influenced by the Chinese. These Sino-Siamese hybrid vessels have come to be referred to as the South China Sea tradition.[18] Southeast Asia contributed the teak timbers, dowel edge-joining and deep V-shaped hull, while China contributed tabernacle mast steps, iron fastenings, bulkheads, an axial rudder and a fully battened rig. Half a dozen South China Sea tradition wrecks have been found off the east coast of Peninsular Malaysia.[19] Some of these may have been bound for Temasek.

We may now conclude that Chinese junks and Southeast Asian traders would have swung alongside a smattering of Arab and Indian dhows in Temasek sea lanes. During the fourteenth century, the Southeast Asians were transitioning from the thousand-year tradition of lashed-lugs to the fabled *jong* that would fascinate the Portuguese upon their arrival. Beyond the fourteenth century, Sino-Siamese hybrid ships arrived with Thai ceramics during the periods in which various Ming emperors had banned Chinese exports. While the numbers were sometimes slashed, smuggling ensured that junks from northern and southern China continued to call into the port of Singapore.

Notes

1. M. Flecker, "The Jade Dragon Wreck: Sabah, East Malaysia", *Mariner's Mirror* 98, no. 1 (2012): 9–29.

2. P.-Y. Manguin, "Southeast Asian Shipping in the Indian Ocean during the First Millennium A.D.", in *Tradition and Archaeology: Early Maritime Contacts in the Indian Ocean*, edited by H.P. Ray and J.-F. Salles (New Delhi, 1996), p. 185.

3. M. Flecker, "The Thirteenth-century *Java Sea Wreck*: A Chinese Cargo in an Indonesian Ship", *Mariner's Mirror* 89, no. 4 (November 2003): 388–404.

4. M. Flecker and Tai Y.S., *The Flying Fish Wreck, Northern Song (960–1127)* (Petaling Jaya: Innovative Media for Five Dynasty Antique, 2019).

5. Flecker, M., "The Lingga Wreck: An Early 12th Century Southeast Asian Ship with a Chinese Cargo", *Southeast Asian Archaeological Reports* (Singapore: NUS Press, 2019), http://epress.nus.edu.sg/sitereports.

6. H. Liebner, "The Siren of Cirebon: A Tenth-Century Trading Vessel Lost in the Java Sea" (PhD thesis, University of Leeds, 2014).

7. M. Flecker, *The Archaeological Excavation of the 10th Century Intan Shipwreck,* BAR International Series 1047 (Oxford: Archeopress, 2002).

8. P.-Y. Manguin, "The Southeast Asian Ship: An Historical Approach", *Journal of Southeast Asian Studies* 11, no. 2 (1980): 267.

9. Manguin, "The Southeast Asian Ship", p. 268.

10. P.-Y. Manguin, "Ships and Shipping in Southeast Asia", Oxford Research Encyclopedias, Asian History, edited by D. Luddens (Oxford University Press, 2017), https://doi.org/10.1093/acrefore/9780190277727.013.30.

11. M. Flecker, "The Origin of the Tang Shipwreck: A Look at its Archaeology and History", in *The Tang Shipwreck: Art and Exchange in the 9th Century,* edited by A. Chong and S.A. Murphy (Singapore: Asian Civilisations Museum, 2017), pp. 22–39.

12. J. Guy, "The Phanom Surin Shipwreck, a Pahlavi Inscription, and their Significance for the History of Early Lower Central Thailand", *Journal of the Siam Society* 105 (2018): 179–96.

13. J. Miksic, *Singapore and the Silk Road of the Sea* (Singapore: NUS Press 2013).

14. 崔勇《广东″南海Ⅰ号″南宋沉船水下考古发掘项目圆满完成》文博中国 [Cui Yong, "Guangdong Nanhai Number One Southern Song Shipwreck Underwater Archaeological Project Completion", Wenbo Zhongguo App], 16 January 2020, http:// https://wemp.app/posts/82c681ba-2d4a-40cb-9877-d2075f12edad (accessed 1 June 2020).

15. Information obtained from a range of Vietnam newspaper reports.

16. M. Flecker, "The Bakau Wreck: An Early Example of Chinese Shipping in Southeast Asia", *International Journal of Nautical Archaeology* 30, no. 2 (2001): 221–30.

17. M. Flecker, "The Binh Thuan Shipwreck", in *The Binh Thuan Shipwreck, Melbourne 1 & 2 March 2004*, Christie's Australia auction catalogue (Victoria: Christie's, 2004), pp. 2–15.

18. M. Flecker, "The South-China-Sea Tradition: The Hybrid Hulls of South-East Asia", *International Journal of Nautical Archaeology* 36, no. 1 (2007): 75–90.

19. R. Brown and S. Sjostrand, *Maritime Archaeology and Shipwreck Ceramics in Malaysia* (Kuala Lumpur: Department of Museums and Antiquities, 2004).

5

The Orang Laut and the *Negara Selat* (Realm of the Straits)

Leonard Y. Andaya

The Orang Laut played a significant role in the history of the Straits. This area is centred on the Straits of Melaka and the islands, the seas and the straits at the northern and southern entrances of the Straits and at the southernmost end of the South China Sea. This world or Realm of the Straits (*Negara Selat*) gained prominence because of the vibrant east–west international maritime trade between Europe, the Middle East, India and Sri Lanka in the west and China, Japan, Korea and the Ryukyu Islands in the east. Southeast Asia lay athwart this trading lane, with the Straits of Melaka being the only known passageway for centuries. Even after the Sunda Straits between Java and Sumatra came to be used increasingly after the sixteenth century, the Straits of Melaka continued to be the most travelled maritime route through Southeast Asia. The waters of the Straits were generally calm, and the mountain chains running along both spines of Sumatra and the Malay Peninsula provided all-year protection from the annual northeast and southwest monsoon winds. Before entering and leaving the southern end of the Straits of Melaka, ships had to cross a dangerous stretch of waters from the southeastern coast of Sumatra to Singapore, the Riau-Lingga Archipelagos and the islands and straits of the southern end of the South China Sea. For this reason, the entire area was considered to be a single maritime unit and came to be referred to simply as "the Sea" or "the Straits".

In the Raffles MS 18 version of the *Sulalatus-Salatin,* more commonly known as the *Sejarah Melayu* or Malay Annals,[1] the Malay word "Laut" or sea is the term used for this maritime space. When the Palembang lord Sri Tribuana decided to leave permanently to go abroad, he said to his minister: "I want to go to the Sea (*Laut*) to look for a good place so I can build a settlement (*hendak berankgkat ke Laut, hendak mencari tempat yang baik hendak beta perbuatkan negeri*)."[2] Once he left Palembang he crossed over to the Sepat Straits and from the Sepat Straits to the Sambar Straits. In another episode in the same text, Melaka had just been conquered by the Portuguese, forcing the sultan to flee. The Melaka Bendahara summoned his son Tun Pikrama and ordered him to "go to the Sea (*Laut*) and gather all the people of the Sea, and then let's go to meet our lord.... And so Tun Pikrama goes and assembles all the peoples of the Sea (*Sakai*) and the *Sakai* gathered together (*Pergi engkau ke Laut, mari kita pergi menjemput Yang Dipertuan ... Maka Tun Pikrama pun pergilah mengimpunkan segala sakai, maka segal sakai pun berkampunglah*).[3] The reference to the area as "Laut" appears to have been noted by others, as early Chinese sources mention an important area, "Lo-yueh", which two French scholars reconstructed as being the Malay word "Laut".[4]

The other term used for this area is *Selat*, or Straits. Arabs write about *Salahit* (from the Malay word "Selat"), which was rich in natural produce and located somewhere on or off the east coast of Sumatra.[5] When Sri Tribuana sailed from Palembang to the *Laut*, he sailed across the Sepat and Sambar Straits, which are just two of the many straits in these waters. While "Laut" appears to be a common reference to the seas inhabited by the Orang Laut, the alternate name "Selat" appears to have been used more frequently in later centuries in the form of *Negara Selat* (Realm of the Straits). In a 1719 Dutch East India Company (VOC) source, a Raja Negara Selat is mentioned as leader of the Orang Laut based in Singapore and head of large numbers of Orang Laut. He led a major part of the Orang Laut in abandoning the Bendahara when he assumed the Johor throne after the 1699 assassination of Sultan Mahmud Syah (*Mangkat di Julang*).[6] In November 1767, Raja Ismail, the exiled contender to the Siak throne, sailed into Riau waters with a fleet comprised mainly of Orang Laut led by the Raja Negara Selat. When Raja Ismail was defeated in his bid to recover his legacy, the Raja Negara Selat and his Orang Laut followers remained loyal and accompanied him to Terengganu, where the Raja Negara Selat died in about 1770.[7] The Raja Negara Selat appears also in Malay texts. In the *Hikayat Siak*

(Cod. Or. 7304, Leiden), the Raja Negara Selat plays a key role in saving the posthumous son of the assassinated Sultan Mahmud Syah of Johor.[8] The late-nineteenth-century *Tuhfat al-Nafis* provides a Bugis slant to events and refers to Sultan Hussein, who was selected by Raffles and the British as the real successor to the Riau-Johor throne in 1819, simply as "*Yang Dipertuan Selat*", or Lord of the Straits.[9] Reference to the entire maritime space at the southern end of the Straits of Melaka as *Negara Selat* befits the concept of a maritime realm, whose importance can be better appreciated from a sea perspective.

A leading proponent of the sea perspective is the Pacific Island or Oceanic scholar Epeli Hau'ofa. He strongly rejects the commonly held perception of the Pacific by outside scholars and international organizations as comprising tiny, isolated and dependent islands within a vast empty ocean. Instead, he presents an insider perspective of the Pacific as a vibrant "sea of islands", crisscrossed by intersecting sea lanes leading to resources and families across this maritime space.[10] The *Negara Selat*, consisting of many small islands, some mere outcrops of rocks, and numerous and often treacherous straits, should be understood in precisely the same manner. Organized ordinarily in small groups under a leader, the Orang Laut of the Negara Selat were a mobile population moving across the sea lanes and maintaining certain islands as burial grounds or sacred sites. The nature of the environment may form obstacles to outsiders, but to its natural inhabitants it is a strength, offering protection and connectivity to groups within and outside the realm. This "sea of islands" consists of many maritime pathways leading to marine products, to family members on different islands and straits, and to the sea markers that form part of the people's access to their history and ancestors. The strength of the Orang Laut derived from their willingness to join with other Orang Laut communities on long collecting expeditions and in war fleets when required. The smallness of the basic socio-economic unit, therefore, belies the power and influence that the Orang Laut exercised in the past. Skilled navigators and fierce fighters, the combined forces of the Orang Laut communities made them formidable allies or foes.

Malay rulers along the Straits of Melaka recognized the value of the Orang Laut as collectors of sea produce for international trade and as an essential naval force. They could guide foreign traders through the difficult waters of the *Negara Selat*, assure the safety of the waterways leading to and from Malay entrepôts, and defend the kingdom from attacks by sea. In the *Suma Oriental*, Pires describes the Orang Laut, "of whom there are a large number in our time [early sixteenth century]", as having also played a part in the defence of Melaka against the Portuguese.[11] Yet, the Orang Laut groups were not monolithic, and even

Figure 5.1

among themselves there was an acknowledged difference in status, based primarily on numbers and the importance of their particular stretch of sea. In the late nineteenth century, the Dutch listed the various tasks the Orang Laut performed for the Johor court. And while the nature of the tasks themselves provided some measure, it was the bride price for women from a particular Orang Laut group that was the decisive evidence of status. Based on this criterion, the Orang Suku Bintan may have been the most prestigious Orang Laut group because its women could demand the highest bride price.[12]

This appears to be in keeping with the documents that mention Bintan as an island of some note. In the thirteenth century the Arab geographer Ibn Said described Bintan as a centre where "armed black pirates with poisoned arrows emerge, possessing armed warships; they plunder people…".[13] Chinese sources cite a trade mission to China from Bintan in 1323, and in the earliest extant recension of the *Sulalatus-Salatin* (Raffles Ms. 18), dated 1612, there is the famous episode where the Palembang lord Sri Tribuana leaves the kingdom and goes to the *Negara Selat*. While en route with his followers he is met by a fleet of four hundred ships from the queen of Bintan and brought to the island, where the queen decides to adopt him as a son. After a while he decides to resettle on Temasek. He thus asks for and receives men, elephants and horses from the queen and goes on to create a city, which he renames Singapura.[14] This episode provides details of Bintan, which clearly marks it as a major centre of the Orang Laut, with a queen and access to many ships and other resources.

The value of the Orang Laut was recognized by ambitious Malay entrepôt states, and thus the Orang Laut were wooed as allies to become the primary naval force to guide ships to port and to maintain peace in the trade lanes. The Orang Laut proved equally useful in providing sea products, such as tortoiseshells, pearls, mother-of-pearl, tripang and edible seaweed, primarily for the China market. This is the reason the Orang Laut are mentioned in Malay, Portuguese and Dutch sources as playing a decisive role in the search by refugee Malay and other local princes for a favourable site to build an entrepôt. To assure the safety of these capitals, they also placed themselves at crucial locations, particularly at the mouths of the rivers, to prevent attacks on the entrepôts. In return for the services they provided to the Malay entrepôt kingdoms, the Orang Laut were assured of a thriving port in which to sell their products and purchase foreign goods. Malay rulers also presented titles and "robes of honour" to the Orang Laut leaders, which were greatly prized because they enhanced the status of their group over other Orang Laut communities.

The earliest evidence of the relationship between the Orang Laut and Malay rulers comes from a southeast Sumatran polity known as Śrīvijaya (late seventh to the fourteenth century). Yijing, the Buddhist monk who travelled to Śrīvijaya in the late seventh century, mentions native pilots who guided Chinese ships through the dangerous waters around Palembang. He called them *"Kunlun"* and described them as "dark and curly-headed". Ming records from the fifteenth century also describe the *Kunlun* guiding Chinese ships through the region (*Negara Selat*) to the Indian Ocean.[15] Chinese descriptions leave little doubt that the *Kunlun* referred to the Orang Laut. When the main settlement of Śrīvijaya was at Palembang up the Musi River, there was an Orang Laut village at Sungsang at the river mouth that was ideally placed to prevent any surprise attack from the sea. After the destruction of the Palembang site by the Cholas in 1025, Śrīvijaya's capital moved north to Jambi. The Orang Laut were found to be settled at Simpang, a village at the junction of the two tributaries that allowed access to the Batang Hari River, which led up to the new capital. The strategic location of the Orang Laut village was not coincidental but was deliberate to enable the Orang Laut to serve as an early warning system in case of attack by sea.

Melaka (circa 1400 to 1511) was the direct successor of Śrīvijaya, and its rapid rise to become a leading entrepôt in the Straits may have been due to the experience that the refugee Malays brought to the new settlement. What strengthens this view is the fact that according to the *Sulalatus-Salatin*, which was written in the Melaka period (despite the earliest extant recension being dated 1612), there is a clear description of the move of the Palembang prince (Sri Tribuana) from Palembang and eventually to Melaka with the help of the Orang Laut. This story is also told in the *Suma Oriental*, an early sixteenth-century account by the Portuguese apothecary Tomé Pires, who was based in Portuguese Melaka between 1512 and 1515. According to this account, when the Portuguese envoys were in Melaka in 1509 they were told that the Laksamana and the Bendahara were the fifth-generation descendants of the Orang Laut leaders.[16] The Orang Laut continued their role as guardians of the trade lanes and as defenders of their Malay ally. When the Portuguese attacked Melaka in 1511, Pires recounts the fierce resistance they encountered from the Orang Laut, "who carry blow-pipes with their small arrows of black hellebore [poisonous plants] which, as they touch blood, kill, as they often did to our Portuguese in the enterprise and destruction of the famous city of Malacca."[17] After Melaka fell, according to the *Sulalatus-Salatin*, the Orang Laut were summoned by a Melaka official to gather and bring the refugee Sultan Mahmud Syah to a new capital.

The story of the Orang Laut in the kingdom of Johor/Riau-Johor (1530s to late nineteenth century) is similar to that in the Śrīvijaya and the Melaka periods. The Orang Laut were directly involved in finding a safe site up the Johor River for the new refugee Melaka ruler, and once again they established themselves on a site at the mouth of the river. For the first time there is also an indication that they may have helped to direct ships to a customs post established by the Malay ruler. In a 1619 Portuguese map, there is a site called "Xabandaria" (Shahbandar's Post) on the eastern side of the island of Singapore facing the river. It was a well-chosen site because it was located just to the east of the Johor River where ships had to make the hazardous crossing through the straits formed by Pedra Branca, Middle Rock and South Ledge.

The Johor regicide in 1699 was a major watershed in relations between the Orang Laut and the Malay kingdoms. The assassination of the Johor ruler is said to have brought an end to the Melaka dynasty, as the Bendahara now assumed the throne. The incident divided the Orang Laut communities, with some remaining faithful to the new dynasty, while others abandoned Johor and sought a new Malay alliance. According to early eighteenth-century Dutch sources, many Orang Laut sought to restore an old alliance with the Palembang ruler. Greatly complicating the already confused situation was the emergence of an individual called Raja Kechil from the Minangkabau community in Siak across the Straits in Sumatra, who claimed to be the son of the murdered Johor ruler. Many of the Orang Laut shifted their allegiance and helped him to seize the throne from the Bendahara. The latter then hired some Bugis refugees in the region as mercenaries, and so there ensued a long conflict that ended with the victory of the Bendahara family and the Bugis. When the Bugis became ensconced in Johor, they replaced the Orang Laut as the major fighting force of the ruler and

Figure 5.2 "Seletars of Singapore".

Figure 5.3 "Malays of the Salat, Malay Peninsula".

made it difficult for the Orang Laut to remain in the kingdom. From this period onward, the Orang Laut were displaced economically and militarily by the Bugis. Johor no longer became the primary focus of Orang Laut loyalty, and different groups came to serve rival kingdoms in Johor, Jambi, Palembang and others. Without the unity of purpose they possessed in the past, the Orang Laut gradually lost their value to the Malay kingdoms.

Equally damaging to the Orang Laut were changes that came to the region. With a dominant position in the Malay Peninsula and Singapore, the British greatly expanded the tin-mining industry with new expensive technology supported mainly by European capital, and they created a rubber industry through systematic experimentation with a plant native to Brazil. In both these industries, Chinese migrant labour continued, while large numbers of Indians were imported to work in the rubber estates. Tin and rubber became the two pillars of the colonial economy, dwarfing the so-called "straits produce", including sea products gathered by the Orang Laut. The role of the Orang Laut as the primary navies of the Malay kingdoms was also weakened considerably with the introduction of steamships and new sea charts pioneered by the British. The Orang Laut were no longer indispensable, and any piratic activities were now severely curtailed as a result of the introduction of steamships and advanced armaments, as well as the signing of the 1824 Anglo-Dutch treaty that divided the Malay world into Dutch and British spheres of influence. Malay rulers were now held accountable for the actions of those living within their borders, including the Orang Laut, and both European colonial powers were quick to complain and seek redress from the Malay rulers. The rules of operation in the waters of the *Negara Selat* had been changed forever, thus undermining the importance of the Orang Laut to the Malay kingdoms.

There was such a precipitous decline in the power and influence of the Orang Laut in the affairs of the region that in the nineteenth century foreign observers characterized them as a shy, elusive and inconsequential sea people. The 1849 sketches of an Orang Laut couple (fig. 5.2) and a Malay family (fig. 5.3) by John Turnbull Thompson (from the University of Otago's Hocken Pictorial Collections) reflect both the changed circumstances of the Orang Laut and European belief in certain "measures of man" that mark a society's place in the stage of human civilization.[18] Among these "measures" was a state of dress or undress of a group, and so one needs to exercise caution in interpreting these images. The Orang Seletar (one Orang Laut group) is depicted with very little clothing, which was an important measure of "civilization". The Malay couple is fully clothed and is obviously regarded as higher up in the civilized scale. As a result of the Orang Laut's prominent role in the trade and politics of the Malay world, even into the nineteenth century, they would have participated in the vibrant cosmopolitan atmosphere of the entrepôts along the Straits of Melaka and enjoyed the variety and sophistication of the textiles from India, the ceramics from China and the armaments from Europe. The physical presence of Malays and the Orang Laut would have been indistinguishable, with the major exception of Muslim women, who covered their breasts. Yet, the European gaze focused on the exotic, the nakedness of the Orang Laut couple, hence revealing the underlying bias of the European gaze.

Even in this brief paper, one can see that the Orang Laut were an indispensable part of the history of the region. Yet they are barely if ever mentioned in the histories of Indonesia, Malaysia or Singapore. There are political reasons for the downplaying or ignoring of the role of the Orang Laut in the histories of Indonesia and Malaysia. In Singapore the neglect is due mainly to the lack of interest until recently in the pre-1819 history of this island state. The decision by the Nalanda-Sriwijaya Centre in the ISEAS – Yusof Ishak Institute to commemorate the bicentenary in 2019 by a series of lectures on the early historical period offers an ideal opportunity to highlight the Orang Laut as an important component not only in the history of Singapore but also of Southeast Asia.

Notes

1. C.C. Brown translated this text into English and called it "Sejarah Melayu or Malay Annals", though the actual manuscript is called *Sulalatus-Salatin*, or "Genealogy of Kings". C.C. Brown, "Sejarah Melayu or Malay Annals", *Journal of the Malayan Branch of the Royal Asiatic Society* 25, nos. 2–3 (1952).

2. Brown, *Sejarah Melayu*, p. 28; Abdul Rahman Haji Ismail, transcriber, "Teks/Text of Raffles MS. No. 18", in *Sejarah Melayu, The Malay Annals*, edited by Cheah Boon Kheng (Kuala Lumpur: Malaysian Branch of the Royal Asiatic Society, 1998), p. 88.

3. Brown, *Sejarah Melayu*, p. 191; Abdul Rahman, "Teks/Text of Raffles MS. No. 18", p. 296. "Sakai" is commonly used in Malay texts to indicate the Orang Laut.

4. O.W. Wolters, *The Fall of Srivijaya in Malay History* (Kuala Lumpur: Oxford University Press, 1970), p. 11.

5. Wolters, *The Fall of Srivijaya*, p. 11.

6. Leonard Y. Andaya, *The Kingdom of Johor: Economic and Political Developments* (Kuala Lumpur: Oxford University Press, 1975), pp. 256, 264.

7. Raja Ali-Haji Ibn Ahmad, *The Precious Gift: Tuhfat al-Nafis*, translated and annotated by Virginia Matheson and Barbara Watson Andaya (Kuala

Lumpur: Oxford University Press, 1982), p. 353, fol. 174n1; p. 354, fol. 178n2.

8. Muhammad Yusoff Hashim, ed., *Hikayat Siak: Dirawikan oleh Tengku Said* (Kuala Lumpur: Dewan Bahasa dan Pustaka, 1992), pp. 113–14.

9. Raja Ali-Haji Ibn Ahmad, *The Precious Gift*, pp. 243–44.

10. Epeli Hauòfa, "Our Sea of Islands", *Contemporary Pacific* 6, no. 1 (1994): 152, 157.

11. Armando Cortesão, ed., *The Suma Oriental of Tomé Pires*, vol. 2 (New Delhi Asian Educational Services, 1990), p. 233.

12. Leonard Y. Andaya, *Leaves of the Same Tree: Trade and Ethnicity in the Straits of Melaka* (Honolulu: University of Hawai'i Press, 2008), pp. 182–84.

13. Wolters, *Fall of Srivijaya*, p. 11.

14. Brown, *Sejarah Melayu*, pp. 28–31.

15. Andaya, *Leaves of the Same Tree*, p. 51.

16. Cortesão, *Suma Oriental*, p. 235.

17. Cortesão, *Suma Oriental*, p. 233.

18. Michael Adas, *Machines as the Measure of Man* (Ithaca: Cornell University Press, 1989), pp. 214–15.

6

Avoidance of Shipwreck in the *Malay Annals*: A Trope in Buddhist Narratives of Maritime Crossings[1]

Andrea Acri

The *Malay Annals* narrate how Sri Tribuana, sailing towards the land of Temasek that he espied while out hunting, was caught in a storm that threatened to wreck his ship. The crew could not bale the water out fast enough and the ship was in danger of being wrecked. Sri Tribuana was asked to throw his heavy crown overboard to lighten the ship. This he did, and the storm abated.[2] The symbolism of this avoidance of shipwreck has not been satisfactorily explained. This essay searches for this symbolism of the avoidance of shipwrecks in Buddhist narratives of maritime crossings.

Seafaring Monks in Maritime Asia[3]

The spread of Buddhism from the Indian Subcontinent to Sri Lanka, Southeast Asia and China via the maritime routes goes back at least to the early centuries of the current era. Historical evidence records a steady traffic of monks travelling both eastwards and westwards along the sea routes linking the swathe of territory between the Indian Subcontinent and Japan. Written and material evidence becomes substantial from the fifth century onwards, testifying to an efflorescence of long-distance

55

maritime contacts across Maritime Asia. This vast geographical expanse of sea and land, largely coinciding with a trans-regional "Buddhist Cosmopolis", became the natural theatre for the journeys of hundreds of travelling monks who crossed the seas far and wide in search of texts, teachers and patrons.[4] The vehicles of their travels were the Monsoon-driven merchant ships that plied the maritime routes connecting a web of entrepôts linking the Indian Ocean to the China Sea, carrying—alongside their valuable cargos—pilgrims, diplomats and religious personalities of disparate affiliations.

Most of the monks travelling in both directions between India and China preferred the maritime route to the overland one, or at least sought to include a maritime leg in their journey, which usually included stopovers in Sri Lanka and the Malay-Indonesian Archipelago. Maritime mobility of Buddhist agents, besides being numerically significant, was also quicker and easier than hitherto assumed. In spite of this, both the Jataka tales and the Sino-Japanese and Tibetan biographies of monks travelling from China to India or vice-versa make clear that travel across the maritime trading channels linking the two regions was not devoid of perils. Besides imagined entities such as marine monsters and other supernatural beings, the most feared hindrances in the minds of the travellers were storms, unfavourable winds, pirates and unskilled or unscrupulous crews.

The earliest account by Faxian (337/342–c.422) recounts his maritime journey from India and Sri Lanka back to China, providing lively details about his momentous voyage on a large, two-hundred-passenger merchant vessel.[5] The ship encounters a storm, probably between Sri Lanka and the Andaman or Nicobar islands, and thanks to the monk's prayers to Guanshiyin/Avalokiteśvara, the vessel, crew and the monk's precious cargo of Buddhist scriptures are saved. Later in his journey the monk risks being thrown overboard by the non-Buddhist crew, and he is saved *in extremis* by his lay supporter (*dānapati*). The account presents a mix of verisimilar and supernatural elements and, interestingly, shares some close parallels with Dharmarakṣa's Chinese translation of the Lotus Sūtra, especially passages dealing with descriptions of perils of the sea and the invocation to Avalokiteśvara.

Similar tropes are echoed in the biographies of Vajrabuddhi (671–741)[6] and Amoghavajra (704–774). Both Vajrabuddhi's and Faxian's accounts narrate about a storm that must have happened in the proximity of Java or Sumatra; they both carried rare Sanskrit texts with them; and they both manage to avert disaster by means of a spell (*dhāraṇī*)—imploring Mahāpratisarā and Guanshiyin/Avalokiteśvara, respectively. Whereas Faxian manages to save all his precious Sanskrit texts, Vajrabuddhi ends up losing some of

Figure 6.1 Model by Nick Burningham of a twelfth-century Southeast Asian lash-lug craft that would have sailed across the Bay of Bengal. (Photo courtesy of Nick Burningham.)

them, including the full version of the *Vajraśekharatantra*. The same circumstance of the recitation of the *Mahāpratisarādhāraṇī* to avert shipwreck while travelling by sea is associated with Vajrabuddhi's disciple Amoghavajra when he was on his way from China to Sri Lanka in 741. While the circumstances narrated in the account may have been based on standard tropes from Chinese hagiographical literature rather than reality, the information found in the Taisho canon that in 758 Amoghavajra actually submitted a copy of the *Mahāpratisarādhāraṇī* to Emperor Suzong to be carried as an amulet confirms that Amoghavajra had access to a version of this text, and transmitted it to China. Furthermore, Chinese sources report that Vajrabuddhi met Amoghavajra in Java.

Both Vajrabuddhi's and Amoghavajra's accounts are similar to that expounded in the fifth narrative in the central and longest text in the Mahāpratisarā corpus, the Sanskrit *Mahāpratisarāvidyārājñī*, in which the merchant Vimalaśaṅkha saves his ship from a storm, lightning and meteors sent by Nāgas. On that occasion, Vimalaśaṅkha writes down the *Mahāpratisarādhāraṇī* and fixes the amulet to the top of a flagstaff. Whether actual or imagined, the above-mentioned accounts speak in favour of the popularity of Mahāpratisarā and the spell she personifies among Buddhist travellers, and they match the material evidence on the propagation of her cult across the Buddhist world via the maritime routes.

The biographies of monks plying the sea routes between India and China from the fifth to the early eleventh century share interwoven aspects of narrative, imagery and factual data with respect to maritime journeys and the avoidance of shipwreck, and they are similar in that they share the trope of the "miraculous response" in Chinese hagiographical literature; i.e., the power intrinsic in some objects and devotional acts, and the intervention of a tutelary deity. These accounts reflect the development across the Buddhist world of "Saviour Cults" focusing on the Bodhisattvas Avalokiteśvara, Tārā and Mahāpratisarā as protectors of travellers, and of sailors in particular, as evidenced by art, material culture and Buddhist canonical and extra-canonical texts.[7]

The imaginary and supernatural elements of avoiding shipwrecks became predominant in the biography of the famous eleventh-century Eastern Indian monk Atiśa (also known as Dīpaṅkaraśrījñāna, 980–1054),[8] who left the subcontinent to study for a few years in Sumatra (or the Malay Peninsula) with Sauvarṇadvīpī-Dharmakīrti and then went to Tibet. Atiśa joined a group of merchants from Nepal sailing to the Golden Island in search of precious stones. He too encounters difficulties during his crossing of the Indian Ocean, namely a storm supernaturally caused by the Hindu god Śiva, who tries to stop him from leaving India to study the dharma. To defeat Śiva and his consort, Atiśa and his disciple Kṣitigarbha manifest themselves as wrathful tantric deities; the latter "launches a preemptive strike against the enemies of Buddhism, including Hindus, Muslims, and practitioners of the Bon religion in Tibet".[9]

Imaginary elements aside, the account of Atiśa's crossing of the sea strikes me as a lively and quite accurate depiction of an actual incident at sea, including descriptions of the massive weights used as anchors to stabilize the ship during the tempest. The detail of throwing overboard anchor-stones fastened to the ship with chains during a storm is also found in the Sanskrit *Kathāsaritsāgara* and the Prakrit *Samāicca Kahā*,[10] and this must have reflected an actual best practice of seamanship.

The section of the account following this contains an elaborate narrative featuring invocations to Raktayamāri, Tārā and Avalokiteśvara, and the transformation of Atiśa and Kṣitigarbha into the Krodha-vighnāntaka deities of Raktayamāri and Acala, respectively. This section resonates with the passages on the conquering of Maheśvara and other harmful beings by protectors of the dharma that we find in Vajrayāna texts. The setting moves from the ocean to the Hindu city of Svabhānātha (perhaps in northern or eastern India), the Turk city in Afghanistan, and Sri Lanka, infested by demon cannibals. After these locations are struck and burnt down by rays emanating from Kṣitigarbha, the two resume their usual human aspect.

The account apparently does not follow factual space and time. All in all, the atmosphere of Atiśa's narrative is quite different from that of the accounts we have examined so far, ridden as it is with supernatural elements; the storm and the danger of the ship being wrecked appear to just be a pretext to attack the enemies of Buddhism, both on the Subcontinent and overseas. Most curious is the detail (repeated twice) that the ship on which Atiśa is travelling is "Nepalese"—an oddity, given that Nepal is a landlocked and predominantly mountainous country. Perhaps we have to understand that a Nepalese party of merchants "chartered" the vessel. Intriguingly, a Newar reminiscence of Atiśa's sea journey to insular Southeast Asia may be the vignette dedicated to an image of the Buddha Dīpaṅkara—also considered the protector of sailors—in Java in the early eleventh-century illustrated manuscript of the *Aṣṭasāhasrikā-Prajñāpāramitā* (cul Add. 1643, folio 2 recto). Further, Sinclair[11] has noted that the identification of an image of the Buddha Dīpaṅkara at Tham Bahī, the monastery founded by Atiśa, with the merchant Siṁhalasārthavāha ("caravan-head Siṁhala") of *Divyāvadāna* 36 etc. may be a vestigial memory of Atiśa's journeys. Thus, the narrative of Atiśa's sea-passage is to be situated in an environment of maritime travel and cultural contacts between the subcontinent/the Himalayan region and Southeast Asia.[12]

The Malay Annals

The preceding accounts of avoidance of shipwrecks in Buddhist narratives of maritime crossings provide a context for the supernatural avoidance of shipwreck found in the 1612 CE recension of the *Malay Annals*, or *Sejarah Melayu* (*Sulalatus-Salatin*), narrating the journey of the ruler of Palembang Sri Tribuana to the island of Bintan in the Riau archipelago and his meeting with Queen Wan Sri Bini. Sri Tribuana's sea voyage is believed to have taken place in the late thirteenth or early fourteenth century; that is, still during the Hindu-Buddhist period, when the East Javanese kingdoms of Singhasari and Majapahit exerted political and cultural influence on Sumatra after the decline of Śrīvijaya.

In chapter 3 of the *Malay Annals*, Sri Tribuana, who has now been adopted as a son by Queen Wan Sri Bini of Bintan, embarks on a hunting trip to Tanjong Bemban and sees Temasek across the water. The *Malay Annals* narrates:

> So Sri Tribuana embarked and started on the crossing. And when they were come out into the open sea, a storm arose and the ship began to fill with water. Bale as they might they could not clear her and the boatswain gave order to lighten the ship. But though much was thrown overboard, they still could not bale the ship dry. She was now close to Telok Blanga, and the boatswain said to Sri Tribuana, "It seems to me,

your Highness, that it is because of the crown of kingship that the ship is floundering. All else has been thrown overboard, and if we do not do likewise with this crown we shall be helpless with the ship." And Sri Tribuana replied "Overboard with it then." And the crown was thrown overboard. Thereupon the storm abated, and the ship regained her buoyance and was rowed to land.[13]

This account of the crossing of the Straits by Sri Tribuana contains some familiar narratological elements: the storm, and the need to jettison the cargo—including the protagonist's crown—to avert being wrecked. Just as Vajrabuddhi loses the precious complete version of the *Vajraśekharatantra*, so Sri Tribuana loses the royal diadem, which, by being thrown overboard, ultimately causes the storm to dissipate and the boat to land safely. It is possible that a literary trope might have been at play in both accounts—the one "magico-ritual", the other (predominantly) "royal". In the case of Vajrabuddhi, as we have seen above, the episode of the loss of the full *Vajraśekhara* could have been dramatized to legitimize the monk as the originator of an esoteric initiatory tradition in a foreign country. In the case of the *Malay Annals*, the detail about Sri Tribuana's royal crown being so "heavy" that it needed to be thrown overboard lest the ship sink suggests the act fulfilled a symbolic and metaphysical aim: before landing in a foreign land and being crowned as its new ruler, the powerful "Stranger King" should be deprived of his sovereignty. It is significant to mention here that Braginsky has detected a nucleus of shared narrative motifs between the *Malay Annals* and other Classical Malay texts, as well as (East) Javanese Pañji romances.[14] Those sources combine the motif of the shipwreck with that of the drowned crown and the prince who is thrown by the waves to the shore of the country, where he marries the local princess and becomes king.[15] In order to do so, the hero often becomes a character of low social status, and then is upgraded to his new kingly status. This basic myth, belonging to an archaic "royal cluster", has been transformed in the course of time under the impact of religious and cultural ideas (Hindu, Buddhist and Islamic).

In view of the above, I think it is not beyond the realm of possibility that the Sri Tribuana episode in the *Malay Annals* could have been inspired by textual accounts or oral narratives popular in Sumatra and Java during the Hindu-Buddhist period. This hypothesis has already been voiced by Braginsky and Wolters,[16] who described the connection of this text and its author (a genealogist/performer) with Śrīvijaya. Like Wolters, Kwa[17] has regarded the *Malay Annals* as a covertly Buddhist text, permeated by a worldview and political ideology stemming from the type of Sanskritic Mahāyāna/Mantranaya Buddhism practised in Śrīvijaya.[18] Furthermore, the text calls Sri Tribuana the "ruler of the whole of Suvarṇabhūmi", and declares him to be the son of San Sapurba, ruler of Palembang, and brother of Sang Maniaka. As noted by Winstedt long ago,[19] the names of these three characters apparently derive from those of the three heavenly nymphs (*apsaras*) Suprabhā, Tilottamā and Menakā featuring in Sanskrit texts such as the *Mahābhārata*, as well as the eleventh-century East Javanese *kakavin Arjunavivāha*, as part of Indra's entourage. Hooker and Hooker[20] argued that "at various times and in a number of places, elements of the *Malay Annals* narrative were selected for incorporation into other narratives and 'localized'", and therefore the various versions of the *Malay Annals* need to be considered in terms of a "larger corpus of narratives, each of which is aligned with some basic tenets of the *Malay Annals* tradition, but which add their own local inputs". As we have seen above, this seems to have also been the case in such narratives as the *Siṁhala Jātaka, Divyāvadāna, Kāraṇḍavyūha*, etc. It may thus be argued that the author(s) of the (various versions of the) *Malay Annals* borrowed the account of avoidance of shipwreck from an earlier source—which might in turn have derived from a Mahāyāna scripture, a Jātaka or even a monks' travelogue—reworking it in an original way and stripping out the Buddhist element so as to suit the Islamic fashion of his/their time. In conclusion, the *Malay Annals* could quite aptly be considered an agglomerative, syncretic and hybrid literary source—a prototypical "creole" text indeed, composed in a geographical milieu that has been the theatre of dynamics of ethnic, linguistic and cultural creolization.

Notes

1. The full article on which this essay draws is in A. Acri, "Navigating the 'Southern Seas', Miraculously: Avoidance of Shipwreck in Buddhist Narratives of Maritime Crossings", in *Moving Spaces: Creolisation and Mobility in Africa, the Atlantic and Indian Ocean*, edited by M. Berthet, F. Rosa, and S. Viljoen (Leiden: Brill, 2019), pp. 50–77.

2. C. C. Brown, "Sějarah Mělayu or 'Malay Annals': A Translation of Raffles MS 18 (in the Library of the R.A.S., London) with Commentary", *Journal of the Malayan Branch of the Royal Asiatic Society* 25, nos. 2–3 (1952), p. 30. The Malay text is at page 91 of *Sejarah Melayu: The Malay Annals, MS Raffles 18, New Romanised Edition*, compiled by Cheah Boon Kheng and transcribed by Abdul Rahman Hj. Ismail, Malaysian Branch of the Royal Asiatic Society reprint no. 17 (Kuala Lumpur: Malaysian Branch of the Royal Asiatic Society, 1998).

3. A. Acri, "Imagining 'Maritime Asia'", in *Imagining Asia: Networks, Actors, Sites*, edited by A. Acri, K. Ghani, M.K. Jha, and S. Mukherjee (Singapore: ISEAS – Yusof Ishak Institute, 2019), pp. 36–59.

4. A. Acri, "Introduction: Esoteric Buddhist Networks along the Maritime Silk Routes, 7th–13th Century AD", in *Esoteric Buddhism in Mediaeval Maritime Asia: Networks of Masters, Texts, Icons,* edited by A. Acri (Singapore: ISEAS – Yusof Ishak Institute, 2016), pp. 1–25.

5. A. Grimes, "The Journey of Fa-hsien from Ceylon to Canton", *Journal of the Malayan Branch of the Royal Asiatic Society* 19, no. 1 (1941), pp. 76–92.

6. J. Sundberg and R. Giebel, "The Life of the Tang Court Monk Vajrabodhi as Chronicled by Lu Xiang: South Indian and Sri Lankan Antecedents to the Arrival of the Buddhist Vajrayana in Eighth Century Java and China", *Pacific World: Journal of the Institute of Buddhist Studies,* 3rd ser. vol. 13 (2011): 129–222.

7. H.P. Ray, "Narratives of Travel and Shipwreck", in *Buddhist Narratives in Asia and beyond: In Honor of HRH Princess Maha Chakri Srindhorn on Her Fifty-fifth Birth Anniversary,* edited by P. Skilling and J. McDaniel (Bangkok: Institute of Thai Studies, Chulalongkorn University, 2012), vol. 2, pp. 47–65.

8. See J.B. Apple, *Atiśa Dīpaṃkara: The Illuminator of the Awakened Mind* (Boulder, CO: Shambhala, 2019) for a biography of Atiśa (pp. 1–76) and a summary and sample of his teachings (pp. 77–250).

9. H. Decleer, "Atiśa's Journey to Sumatra", in *Buddhism in Practice,* edited by D.S. Lopez (Princeton, NJ: Princeton University Press), p. 532.

10. D. Schlingloff, *Studies in the Ajanta Paintings: Identifications and interpretations* (Delhi: Ajanta Publications, 1988), pp. 99, 212n107.

11. I. Sinclair, *The Appearance of Tantric Monasticism in Nepal: A History of the Public Image and Fasting Ritual of Newar Buddhism, 980–1380* (PhD dissertation, Monash University, Melbourne, 2016), p. 165.

12. Recently, Sinclair (*Tantric Monasticism in Nepal,* pp. 164–66) has argued that the eight-armed form of Amoghapāśa (whose earliest representations come from the Śrīvijayan domains) in the Thaṃ Bahī monastery in Nepal could have been introduced in memory of its founder Atiśa, and specifically to remember his journey to the Golden Isles, many years after the fact. Both Atiśa and Sauvarṇadvīpī-Dharmakīrti were fervent devotees of Tārā, whose cult was widespread in maritime Southeast Asia and may have been popularized in Tibet by Atiśa after his stay in Sumatra or the Malay Peninsula.

13. Brown, "Sĕjarah Mĕlayu".

14. V. Braginsky, *The Heritage of Traditional Malay Literature: A Historical Survey of Genres, Writings and Literary Views* (Leiden: KITLV Press, 2004), pp. 119–126; V. Braginsky, *Turkic-Turkish Theme in Traditional Malay Literature: Imagining the Other to Empower the Self* (Leiden: Brill, 2015), p. 94n35.

15. The texts from Sumatra and the Malay Peninsula include the *Tambo Minangkabau* (shipwreck in Singapore Straits, lost crown, recovery under the sea, Braginsky 2015, pp. 107–8; crown lost and retrieved in the sea of Sri Lanka, ibid., pp. 93–94); the *Sejarah Melayu* (shipwreck and recovery of

young prince by toddy tapper from Majapahit, Brown, "Sejarah Melayu", pp. 72–75); *Hikayat Merong Mahawangsa* (prince survives shipwreck, Braginsky, *Turkic-Turkish Theme*, p. 113); and *Hikayat Hang Tuah* (king of Melaka and Hang Tuah simultaneously lose their crown and kris in the sea, ibid., pp. 94n35, 153n53).

16. See O.W. Wolters, *The Fall of Śrīvijaya in Malay History* (London: Lund Humphries, 1970), especially chapter 8.

17. Kwa Chong Guan, "Singapura as a Central Place in Malay History and Identity", in *Singapore from Temasek to the 21st Century: Reinventing the Global City*, edited by Karl Hack and Jean-Louis Margolin, with Karine Delaye (Singapore: NUS Press, 2010), pp. 133–54.

18. It is worth stressing that the Śrīvijaya thalassocracy in Sumatra hosted renowned centres of Buddhist activity and higher learning by the seventh century, as documented by Chinese monk Yijing, who praised the high level of Buddhist scholarship he found there, where he stopped—en route from Guangzhou to Nālandā and from there back to China—to read Sanskrit Sūtras. The high level of scholarship and sustained royal sponsorship is confirmed by the evidence of the study of the abstruse Prajñāpāramitā and Abhisamayālaṃkāra literature, as well as the figures of Shihu/*Dānapāla (d. 1018), an exceptionally prolific monk-translator who in the late tenth century reached China with a good knowledge of the languages of Sanfochi/Śrīvijaya and Shepo/Java and of the distinguished Sauvarṇadvīpī-Dharmakīrti, who was Atiśa's mentor for over a decade. Tansen Sen, *Buddhism, Diplomacy, and Trade: The Realignment of Sino-Indian Relations, 600–1400* (Honolulu: Association for Asian Studies and University of Hawai'i Press, 2003), p. 384; C.D. Orzech, *"Translation of Tantras and Other Esoteric Buddhist Scriptures"*, in *Esoteric Buddhism and the Tantras in East Asia*, edited by C.D. Orzech, H.H. Sorensen, and R.K. Payne (Leiden: Brill, 2011), pp. 449–50.

19. R.O. Winstedt, ed., "The Malay Annals or Sejarah Melayu, the earliest Recension from MS. No. 18 of the Raffles Collection, in the Library of the Royal Asiatic Society, London", *Journal of the Malayan Branch of the Royal Asiatic Society* 24, no. 3 (1938): 2.

20. V.M. Hooker and M.B. Hooker, *John Leyden's Malay Annals, Introductory Essay*, reprint 20 (Kuala Lumpur: Malaysian Branch of the Royal Asiatic Society, 2001), p. 40.

7

The Inception of Lion City

Iain Sinclair[1]

In order to understand the nature of a city, it is necessary to understand its founding moment, according to classicists.[2] The traditional account of the founding of pre-colonial Singapura is famously related in the *Sejarah Melayu* literature. Prince Sang Nila Utama sailed to the coast of Temasek, glimpsed a powerful beast there—likened to a lion by bystanders—and was inspired to build "Lion City". Two points will be made here regarding the significance of this often misunderstood episode. Firstly, the city was founded at a place and time that show it to have intruded on a community existing nearby. Secondly, the city's rulers justified their legitimacy by drawing on the South Asian trope of an animal that reveals a charmed place for a settlement.

Temasek's Geographic and Temporal Extent

The traditional account of Singapore's founding leaves out an important part of the picture: people were already living on the island. It is well known that Singapura was founded in a place called Temasek, but here it will be argued that Temasek had its own pre-existing settlement, which was not much older than the new city. What does Temasek include, and when and why did it become known by that name?

There is no record of Temasek before the year 1225, when Zhao Rukuo wrote about a place called Lengga Entrance 凌牙门 (foreign terms transcribed on voyages from Fujian are conveyed here in Hokkien pronunciation[3]). This trading post is usually identified with the Lengga Entrance 龙牙门, Longyamen, documented in 1350 in Wang Dayuan's *Description of the Barbarians of the Isles*. Wang's statement that this place is occupied by natives of Temasek (Tanmasek 单马锡) allows it to be recognized as the western entrance of Telok Blangah, present-day Keppel Harbour.[4] The entrance was once marked by a tall sea stack, resembling a *lingga*, which is presumably the basis for the name Lengga. This is the place where Sang Nila Utama came ashore, according to tradition, after losing his crown on the sea journey from Batam.[5] According to Zhao, it would have been a thriving shipping lane for decades before Sang Nila Utama arrived in the 1290s. But this is not where the prince has his fateful animal encounter and builds a city. That takes place at Kuala Temasek and the Padang, the present-day Fort Canning and Civic District area, a good distance from Telok Blangah (fig. 7.1).

Temasek includes, in addition to Telok Blangah, the "cotton-white" coastline seen by Sang Nila Utama from the heights of Batam. Here Temasek is explained by the royal entourage to be "the end of the mainland" (*ujong tanah besar*) of the Malay Peninsula. This old designation, strictly speaking, ought to encompass the southernmost part of the mainland proper and Johor. The northern limit of Temasek

Figure 7.1 Charles Dyce, "Batu Blair", depicting the western entrance to Telok Blangah, Singapore, and its upright sea stack, 1846. National University of Singapore Museum S1970-0052-047-0. (National University of Singapore Museum Collection.)

is not defined. In period sources, Temasek is never called an island, nor is it treated as wholly separate from the Malay Peninsula. There is positive evidence of this in the so-called Mao Kun map associated with the Treasure Voyages of the fifteenth century. This map shows Temasek (Tammasek 淡马锡) to be contiguous with the mainland, in the view of Mills.[6] Although Wheatley's reading of the map is quite different,[7] it too does not find the mainland to be separate from Temasek.

Temasek emerges into history between 1278 and 1293, during the reign of Trần Nhân Tông. At this time envoys of Temasek were in Vietnam seeking diplomatic recognition. They spoke a "foreign" language. The last dated reference is from the Old Javanese *Deśavarṇana* 14.2c, written in 1365. The *Deśavarṇana* refers to Tumasik as one of several Malay polities located on the Peninsula. Although documents from the Ming dynasty Treasure Voyages refer to Temasek, they most likely do so to preserve backward compatibility with Wang Dayuan's *Description*.

As for Singapura itself, period Chinese sources do not know any place in the region by this name. The city founded in Temasek must have acquired this name just before being destroyed in the 1380s or thereabouts. Singapura only starts to be mentioned in colonial documents of the early sixteenth century. By then the site of the old dynastic seat, long gone, "is nothing much", having become a mere customs post of the Malacca and Johor Sulanates.

The Date of the Literary Temasek

While the scant historical sources on Temasek have received intense scrutiny, literary works that refer to Temasek have been overlooked. Temasek is mentioned as having a warrior caste (*satria*) in Malay epics such as the *Hikayat Galuh Digantung*. Here Temasek is named as a supplier of forces for joint military campaigns, together with the *satria Nusantara* and others. The queen of Temasik, addressed as Ratu or Permaisuri, is a recurring character in the *Hikayat Panji Jayeng Kusuma*. And in the Old Javanese *Kidung Sunda*, Tumasik is repeatedly named along with other kingdoms as a vassal of Majapahit.[8] There have been few attempts to mine these works for sociocultural information or to determine the circumstances of their authoring. They show, if anything, that Temasek's outsized presence in the regional imagination was not confined to the *Sejarah Melayu*.

A detailed tale of Temasek, yet to be studied in depth, is told in the *Hikayat Panji Kuda Semirang*. In this story the protagonist is incarnated in a Tumasik populated by hill tribes (*orang gunung*), village chiefs (*petinggi desa*) and market traders (*orang pasar*). One of his companions is Demang Singabuwana, "chamberlain" of a place that sounds like a palace. There is again a Ratu Tumasik who is addressed as Permaisuri.

Many aspects of the local scene are repeated in the description of Angkor, which is the next setting in the story. The author may have had little access to specific information about these places, but in any case knows Temasek to be bigger than a city-state.

The general picture gleaned from these literary works is consistent with that of the *Sejarah Melayu*, which likewise mentions Singapura's warriors, marketplace (*pekan*), palace (*istana*) and so on. Yet they are not known to have drawn on the *Sejarah Melayu* literature; they take place in a pre-Islamic Malayo-Javanese world. These literary Hikayats are unaware of Malacca, for the most part, which indicates that their vision of Temasek was formed in a period before the end of the fourteenth century. This is consistent with other sources.

Timah and the Etymology of *Temasek*

The designation Temasek is only attested from the late thirteenth century onwards. Does it reflect some new development occurring at that time? The etymology of *temasek* has not been satisfactorily explained. Rouffaer's derivation of *t-em-asik* from *tasik* + infix *em*, meaning "in the sea",[9] has become a standard explanation. This is an allowable word formation in some Malayo-Polynesian languages,[10] but it is not known whether place names were formed in this way in the Straits region. If so, expressions in late Hikayats such as *rakyat tumasik*—analogous to Chinese expressions such as "Tanmasek natives" 单马锡番—would, taken literally, mean "nation/people in the sea". They could aptly describe the *orang laut* stilt house settlements that long stood in the waters of Telok Blangah. However, a place believed to mean "In the Sea" would have no particular relevance to Singapore or any other island in an archipelago full of islands. And in the relatively early *Sejarah Melayu*, Temasek is referred to as a place name, not an adjective. It has also been pointed out that outsiders may not have perceived Temasek to be a single island surrounded by the sea.

Gerini proposed that the word *timah*, "tin", is incorporated in the name of Temasek.[11] *Timah* is the word for tin in much of the Malayo-Javanese world. Tin ingots had been produced and traded in the region since ancient times, as the findings of maritime archaeology have confirmed[12] (fig. 7.2). Concave ingots of "scoop tin" (*tau sek* 斗锡, *tampang*) were traded at Lengga Entrance, according to Wang Dayuan.[13] Tin was a vital part of Malacca's economy from the start, so the tin trade there would have directly continued Temasek's trade. Tomé Pires knew *timah* to be a metonym for tin-producing regions,[14] and some of these regions, including Perak, Kedah and Selangor (according to Pires), are still putatively named after metal commodities. The fact that all Chinese spellings of Temasek end with the character for "tin", pronounced *sek* 锡

Figure 7.2 Concave tin ingots salvaged from the Intan shipwreck, 10th century. (Original photograph © Michael Flecker.)

in Hokkien, provides solid support for an etymology involving *timah*. Could the word Temasek itself be a Chinese coinage meaning "(where) *timah* (means) tin"?

The hill of Temasek marked on the Mao Kun map is "unquestionably" Bukit Timah, in the view of Gerini. This hill has the highest natural elevation in Singapore and is located in the middle of the island. It is still visible from the ocean in the Pandan Strait area near Keppel Harbour. For Gerini, Temasek is synonymous with Bukit Timah and the island as a whole. Bukit Timah has no known tin deposits, so its unique name—attested with this spelling in the earliest maps of the interior[15]—would have come from another association with tin. Perhaps the profile of the hill was seen by mariners as the chief landmark of a peninsula or an island known for trading in tin.

An unusual feature of the local economy noticed by outsiders was the use of tin currency. The first sultanates established in the Malay world continued the old practice of accepting and minting tin coins.[16] The name of this coinage soon entered Portuguese and Chinese lexicons: "cash" (*caixa*, *kasit* 加失[17]). The Arabic word for a coining die and, by extension, a currency protocol, is *sikka*. It might then be ventured that Arabic *sikka* (Anglicised as "chick" in British India) supplies the -*sek*/-*sik* element of Temasek. Did Muslim traders, arriving in increasing numbers throughout the thirteenth century,[18] start talking about a *timah sikka* region—a literal land of cash? Questions of etymology are hard to settle without adequate grounding in a corpus. However, if Temasek's name is found to have Chinese or Arabic elements, there will be another indication that Temasek emerged along with new growth in long-distance trade.

Singapura's Founding and the Trope of the Valiant Beast

Tales of animals revealing a lucky spot for a new settlement are common in South Asian histories. The general pattern is: The founder looks for a place to settle, he sees a meek animal showing surprising strength there, he then accepts the site for its special qualities. This pattern, the trope of the Valiant Beast, was noticed by the late Simon Digby to feature in the founding myths of medieval cities in India, including Ahmednagar, Almora and Bidar.[19] Sang Nila Utama's sighting of the "powerful" animal on the Padang, the belief among onlookers that the animal resembled a lion, and the subsequent founding of a city on the spot all conform to the trope. Although lions were not a native species in the Malay Archipelago, they were not at all foreign to the culture of the region at the time. Lions are common guardian figures in pre-Islamic Malay Sumatran architecture, and figures directly identifiable as *singha*s are depicted on Javanese zodiac beakers bearing fourteenth-century dates (fig. 7.3).

The animal seen on the Padang is described as having a reddish body, black head and white breast, as displaying great vitality, and as being a bit larger than a he-goat. The description of this animal is identical in all of its tellings, while the discussions about the animal vary. The description must then belong to the older strata of the story. It may also preserve a memory of an actual incident. There is at least one mammal in the local biosphere that matches the description in every respect—namely, the masked palm civet (*Paguma larvata*). It can be imagined that the founders of Singapura should have been able to identify civets, but this is immaterial for the purposes of telling a classical founding story. The trope demands that the valiant beast reveals surprising strength, so the animal cannot be identified as a known predator, such as a civet. Malay writings treat civets as cunning and "vicious" (*marah*) animals, as for instance in the *Cerita 'Pa Musang*.[20] For the same reason, the strange and elusive animal seen on the Padang could not have been a tiger. Of course, tigers were common in Singapore[21] and the Malay Peninsula, and Sang Nila Utama's party can be assumed to have been able to recognize one easily.

The felid seen at the Padang has to remain unidentified in the city's origin story so that it can be recognized as a proverbial lion—a Valiant Beast that is a good omen for the new settlement. The early tellings of the animal encounter would have been limited to justifying the Kuala Temasek–Padang area as the best place to settle. Later, as the settlement developed and took on the name Singapura, the story was retconned in order to liken the animal on the Padang to a *singha*. The subtext is that the Telok Blangah area was less preferable, and probably not even available, to be settled by Sang Nila Utama.

Aspects of the Lion City's founding story are paralleled in the dynasty's re-emergence in Malacca. While it has long been recognized that Malacca's founding myth resembles that of Singapura, it should now be made clear that both stories draw on a common pan-Asian trope, not necessarily from each other. In the Malaccan setting, the future king comes to a spot where a meek animal, an albino mousedeer, kicks

Figure 7.3 (a) Drawing of a Javanese zodiac beaker (British Museum 1859,1228.139) dated 1329, 19th century. (b) Detail showing Virgo, Leo and Cancer, British Museum 1939,0311,0.7.107. (© The Trustees of the British Museum. All rights reserved.)

away his hunting dogs. The king realizes that "this is a good spot" (*baik tempat ini*) for a defensible settlement. The place is then named Malacca because a so-called *kayu melaka*, a myrobalan tree, was growing there. This is a typical Valiant Beast episode, but its specifics derive not from the founding myth of Singapura but from the myth of Vijayanagara.[22] This South Indian kingdom is repeatedly mentioned in connection with Singapura in the *Sejarah Melayu*. The first king of Vijayanagara is said to have built his city at a place where his hunting dogs were bitten by a timid animal, a hare. Vijayanagara's founding notionally took place in 1336, as recounted in two inscriptions of doubted veracity and a third recently discovered inscription,[23] all bearing equivalent dates. The Vijayanagara versions of the story bring out the essential Puranic idea of the place charmed by the gods since time immemorial.

Portuguese trader Fernão Nunes heard the story involving the "mystic hare" at Vijayanagara in about 1535.[24] Tomé Pires had already come across a similar story in connection with Malacca by 1515. Pires, referring to the mousedeer as "an animal like a hare", understood that the Valiant Beast was a portent for a place that favoured its defender.[25] But by the logic of the trope, Malacca should have been named after the mousedeer, not the tree. The Portuguese had also heard that the word *melaka* meant "hidden fugitive" (*furtado fugido*), "banished man". This calls to mind Old Javanese *maleca*, "lowly, outcast(e)", i.e., Sanskrit *mleccha*.[26] If the *negeri melaka* was at first known as a "town of the outcaste", it would have benefited from rebranding along classical lines.

The Lion, the Lion Throne and the Name of Singapura

Singa means "lion"; *pura* means "walled settlement", "city". Where does the name of Singapura come from if not from the sighting of a lion-like animal at its founding? The importance of Singapura, in the context of the *Sejarah Melayu*'s throughline, is that it is the first purpose-built dynastic seat. Singapura is both the creation of the Tribuanic kings and the only place that serves as their base from its beginning to its end. As for the lion, its most definite association on the linguistic and the conceptual levels is with the lion throne dais, the *singgasana*. The lion throne is a perennial symbol of rulership throughout the Sanskritic world. To give a pertinent example, the rulers of fourteenth-century Vijayanagara are valorized as occupants of the *siṃhāsana*.[27]

The lion throne features in the oldest Malay literature and the *Sejarah Melayu*. In the coronation ceremony that inaugurates the dynasty in Palembang, the lion throne takes centre stage. The *siṃhāsana* is mentioned explicitly as the ruler's seat in the *ciri*,[28] the Sanskrit proclamation spoken at this model coronation, and then again at the founding of Singapura. These acts are formal declarations of sovereignty. They invoke the divine right of kings to rule, which the pre-Singapura population of Temasek presumably lacked. The Lion City, unlike the nearby settlements bereft of Sanskritic titles and rulership, has a lion throne. So the most straightforward interpretation is that Singapura designates the "royal burgh". As the *siṃhāsana* is such a clear-cut synecdoche for the king and, by extension, the king's compound, it might be asked whether any walled royal settlement could be called a *siṃhapura*. It has been observed that there were other Siṃhapuras in fourteenth-century South and Southeast Asia, but this observation has not in itself clarified whether *siṃhapura* was a generic designation, nor has it revealed what kinds of contacts, if any, existed between these similarly named cities. The rationale for naming Temasek's royal city may ultimately go back to the dynasty's self-styled roots among the Coḷa kings. Some of these kings' names include the element *keśarin*, "mane-haver"; i.e., lion.[29]

Figure 7.4 Gold armlet with lionesque motif (detail), 14th century, National Museum of Singapore A-1570-A. (Courtesy of the National Museum of Singapore, National Heritage Board.)

The name and image of the lion was certainly tied to fourteenth-century Singapura in the world outside the narrative of the *Sejarah Melayu*. Portuguese observers said that one of the Singapura kings had the moniker "Lion". João de Barros reported that the penultimate ruler of the city was called Sang Singha (*Sangefinga de Cingápura*).[30] The corresponding ruler in the *Sejarah Melayu* is only given the Sanskritic title Paduka Seri Maharaja. He was known as the Sang Aji of Singapura (*sam agy de symgapura*) to Tomé Pires.[31] These sources, if they accurately reflect period usage, show that the royal person and the royal city had taken the same "lion" name by the third quarter of the fourteenth century. The Portuguese were well aware that Singapura had been a major port city with a ruler before they arrived in the region. As such, Barros's etymology "wrong stopover" (*falsa demora*, **singgah-pura*[32]), and other varying attempts to grasp the toponomy of the Singapore Strait in the early colonial period, are at odds with established usage.

A tangible link between the old city and the figure of the lion is demonstrated by the famous gold armlet unearthed from Fort Canning (fig. 7.4). Its design was inaccurately described as that of a "Javanese kala" in Winstedt's excavation report.[33] Winstedt says that the ornament's "lower jaw is missing", as is required in depictions of the self-devouring *kāla* monster, but two parts of the mandible as well as the tongue are clearly visible. The features of the face that Winstedt calls "horns"—as seen in Javanese art of the period—have a definite ear shape. Whereas the *kāla* and *singha* motifs were often confused and distorted in period art, the armlet boasts a relatively naturalistic depiction of a lion-like animal. This most important artefact, recovered intact from a jar buried in the royal compound, is in a category apart from the mass of fragments dug up from Civic District disposal sites. It may be the very face of the Lion City.

Concluding Remarks

Temasek was a fledgling polity in the thirteenth century, born out of new trade arriving from India and China. Its name most likely reflects foreign traders' perceptions of the local economy. The stories of Sang Nila Utama arriving at Temasek without a crown, then seeing an animal that shows where a strong city can be founded, are conveyed in mythic frames that appealed to period audiences. However, the mythic frames may have camouflaged a real legitimation crisis, which seems to have been brought on by an outsider's claim to rule. A tale of two cities is emerging: Telok Blangah, Temasek's prior settlement, poised at a lucrative maritime crossroads, still unstudied by archaeologists; and Singapura, the newer seat of Indo-Malay kings, which superseded Temasek and got to write its own history. The dynamics behind the inception of Lion City are just beginning to be revealed.

Notes

1. This essay is an updated summary of the Singapore's Pasts lecture. References in the notes are limited to secondary sources discussed in the main text and to primary sources not mentioned in the lecture. Additional references are given in the lecture slides archived at the ISEAS – Yusof Ishak Institute. I thank Fong Sok Eng, Andrea Acri, Kwa Chong Guan and lecture attendees for feedback. Asterisks (*) denote artificial expressions.

2. Niccolo Machiavelli, *The Prince and the Discourses* (New York: Carlton House, 1900), pp. 106ff.

3. See Tai Yew Seng, "Zheng He's Navigation Methods and His Visit to Longyamen, Singapore", in the present volume.

4. Roland Braddell, "Lung-ya-men and Tan-ma-hsi", *Journal of the Malayan Branch of the Royal Asiatic Society* 23, no. 1 (1950): 37–51, reprinted in Kwa Chong Guan and Peter Borschberg, eds., *Studying Singapore* (Singapore: NUS Press), pp. 34ff.

5. See Andrea Acri, "Avoidance of Shipwreck in the *Malay Annals*", in the present volume.

6. J.V. Mills, "Malaya in the Wu-Pei-Chih Charts", *Journal of the Malayan Branch of the Royal Asiatic Society* 15, no. 3 (1937): 21–27, https://www.jstor.org/stable/41559895.

7. Paul Wheatley, *The Golden Khersonese* (Kuala Lumpur: University of Malaya Press, 1961), p. 95.

8. C.C. Berg, "Kidung Sunda", *Bijdragen tot de taal-, land- en volkenkunde van Nederlandsch-Indië* 83 (1927): 1–181, verses 1b, 54b, 65a, https://doi.org/10.1163/22134379-90001506.

9. G.P. Rouffaer, "Was Malaka Emporium vóór 1400 A.D., genaamd Malajoer?", *Bijdragen Bijdragen tot de taal-, land- en volkenkunde van Nederlandsch-Indië* 77 (1921): 75, https://doi.org/10.1163/22134379-90001600. Rouffaer nonetheless thought *temasik* should mean "[a place] in [ancient] Samudra [Sumatra]".

10. For example, Pedro Serrano Laktaw, *Diccionario Tagálog-Hispano* (Manila: Islas Filipinas, 1914), p. 1322.

11. G.E. Gerini, "The Nāgarakretāgama List of Countries on the Indo-Chinese Mainland (*circâ* 1380 A.D.)", *Journal of the Royal Asiatic Society of Great Britain and Ireland* (1905): 500–511, https://doi.org/10.1017/S0035869X00033517.

12. Michael Flecker, *The Archaeological Excavation of the 10th Century Intan Shipwreck* (Oxford: Archaeopress, 2003), pp. 63–65, 81–82.

13. Tai Yew Seng, email, 12 October 2018.

14. Tomé Pires, *The Suma Oriental of Tomé Pires*, vol. 2, translated and edited by Armando Cortesão (London: Hakluyt Society, 1944), pp. 260, 489–90.

15. James Franklin, "A Chart of the Island of Singapore" (Nationaal Archief, 1822), consulted at the *On Paper: Singapore before 1867* exhibition at the

National Library of Singapore, 17 October 2019. A proposed original spelling, *bukit temak, is not attested.

16. Jorge Manuel dos Santos Alves, "Gold and Tin Coinage in the Sultanates of Northern Sumatra (14th–16th Centuries)", in *Poids et mesures en Asie du Sud-Est*, edited by Pierre le Roux, Bernard Sellato, and Jacques Ivanoff (Paris: École française d'Extrême-Orient, 2004), pp. 98ff.

17. J.V.G. Mills, "Ma Huan's Contribution to the 'Hobson-Jobson' of Yule and Burnell", *T'oung Pao*, 2nd ser. vol. 61, no. 1 (1975): 149, https://doi.org/10.1163/156853275X00035.

18. Geoff Wade, "Islam across the Indian Ocean to 1500 CE", in *Early Global Interconnectivity across the Indian Ocean World*, edited by Angela Schottenhammer, vol. 2 (Cham: Palgrave Macmillan, 2019), pp. 91–92, 105–6, https://doi.org/10.1007/978-3-319-97801-7_5.

19. Simon Digby, "Travels of the Acaryas in the Sixteenth Century according to Taranatha", unpublished correspondence with David Templeman, 28 November 2004.

20. R.O. Winstedt, "Father Civet", *Journal of the Straits Branch of the Royal Asiatic Society* 50 (1908): 88, https://www.jstor.org/stable/41561694.

21. Marsita Omar, "Tigers in Singapore", *Singapore ɲnfopedia*, [2007], https://eresources.nlb.gov.sg/infopedia/articles/SIP_1081_2007-01-17.html.

22. Pushkar Sohoni, "The Hunt for a Location: Narratives on the Foundation of Cities in South and Southeast Asia", *Asian Ethnology* 77 (2018): 220ff, https://asianethnology.org/downloads/ae/pdf/AsianEthnology-2116.pdf.

23. Srinivas Ritti, *Inscriptions of the Vijayanagara Rulers*, vol. 6, *Sanskrit Inscriptions* (Bengaluru: Indian Council of Historical Research, 2017), pp. xxvii, 8–12.

24. H. Heras, *Beginnings of Vijayanagara History* (Bombay: Indian Historical Research Institute, 1929), pp. 1ff.

25. Pires, *Suma Oriental*, vol. 2, pp. 236–37.

26. P.J. Zoetmulder, *Old Javanese Dictionary*, vol. 1 (Leiden: KITLV, 1982), pp. 1094, 1144.

27. Ritti, *Inscriptions of the Vijayanagara Rulers*, 18ff.

28. Ahmat Adam, ed., *Sulalat u's-Salatin* (Kuala Lumpur: Yayasan Karyawan, 2016), pp. 374–75.

29. The connection between Siṃhapura and regnal names such as Keśarī or Parakeśarī was pointed out to me by Nalina Gopal (28 August 2019).

30. João de Barros, *Segunda decada da Asia*, Livre 6 ([Lisbon:] Impressa per Germão Galharde de Lixboa, 1553), p. 77.

31. Pires, *Suma Oriental*, vol. 2, pp. 231, 466. Malay *sang aji* conveys the same sense as Sanskrit *pāduka-śrīmahārāja*.

32. Gerini, "The Nāgarakretāgama List", p. 506n1: "this term is certainly not Malay".

33. R.O. Winstedt, "Gold Ornaments Dug Up at Fort Canning, Singapore", *Journal of the Malayan Branch of the Royal Asiatic Society* 6, no. 4 (1928): 3.

8

A Note on Amoghapāśa-Lokeśvara in Singapura[1]

Kwa Chong Guan

Is the *Sulalatus-Salatin*, or the *Malay Annals/Sejarah Melayu* as Stamford Raffles and John Leyden have popularized the text, an anecdotal history of the Melaka and Johor sultanates, in perhaps ways not too different from Charles Buckley's 1902 *Anecdotal History of Old Times in Singapore*, which is still referred to today? Or is the *Sulalatus-Salatin* a literary text to be read and interpreted within the genres of Malay literature and literary structures for these differing genres of literature? Winstedt led a pioneering generation of scholars to historically differentiate these genres of Malay literature evolving from folk literature through Hindu- and Javanese-influenced genres to culminate in Islamic literature,[2] and sought to read the *Sulalatus-Salatin* as a historical chronicle. Today we are breaking away from Winstedt's search for "objective vocabulary" in the Malay literary texts to studying the structuralist poetics of Malay literature[3] and reconstructing the literary systems framing classical Malay literature.[4]

This note assumes the historicity of Melaka's founding by Iskandar Shah as claimed in the *Sulalatus-Salatin*, and that he is identical with the *Paramjçura* the Portuguese recorded as the founder of the city they conquered, and the *Pai-li-mi-su-la* who the Ming records state lead a mission to China in 1411.[5] The issue of this note is how were the circumstances of Melaka's founding by Iskandar Shah to be recollected and recorded in the *Sulalatus-Salatin*? Could the tragic beginning of Melaka—which Alfonso de Albuquerque and other Portuguese officials learnt from their local informants, that the city they conquered was established by a renegade prince, a *Paramjçura*, who fled his home Palembang after an abortive rebellion against his Javanese overlords and sought refuge in Temasek, where he assassinated his host, and had to again flee—be an auspicious start for a rising Melaka?

The narrator of what was to become the *Sulalatus-Salatin* had the challenging task of writing contemporary history that he and his listeners experienced or would be aware of some thirty years earlier. The first six chapters of the *Sulalatus-Salatin* are therefore read as an intent to rectify this tragic beginning of Melaka with a more befitting genealogy for the founder of Melaka and his descendants.

This note takes off from Oliver W. Wolters's[6] insight into the intentions of the 1436 Melaka genealogist to provide his sultan with an impeccable genealogy by examining the intertextuality of metaphors, metonyms, synecdoches, ironies and other tropes that the genealogist could draw upon, which sought an alternative origin of Melaka to the one in the social memories of the people of Melaka that the Portuguese had recorded some eighty years later. This note seeks out the tropes that the genealogist alluded to in his attempt to assure his audience there was a deeper reality concealed in their social memories of the founding of Melaka. The *Sulalatus-Salatin*, this note suggests, concealed the good news it proclaims in an interrelated series of micro-plots about Sri Tribuana that prefigures Melaka's present.

Wolters has attempted to reconstruct how the "genealogist" at the Melaka *istana* in 1436 provided his sultan with an impeccable genealogy in which Melaka's founder, Sultan Iskandar Shah, was a mime of a Sri Tribuana, Lord of the Three Worlds, a descendent of the eleventh-century Chola kings who raided Śrīvijaya and, further, a descendant of Alexander the Great, and was consecrated as a Bodhisattva in an *abhiṣeka* ritual before he departed Palembang to arrive at Temasek.

The people of Melaka would be aware that the title of their founder, Parameswara, is a Majapahit court title (of Indic origin) awarded to men who married women of higher royal status or became prince consorts. The founder of Melaka could have been a noble-born Javanese or perhaps a Malay taken into the Majapahit court, and then appointed to administer the rump of old Śrīvijaya that Majapahit controlled. This would probably have been before the 1389 civil war, or *paragreg*, that broke Majapahit. Parameswara may have taken the opportunity of this civil war to declare his independence from Majapahit, underestimating the empire's determination and capability to despatch a force to crush him.

As a young man in Palembang, Parameswara would have personally observed or learnt of the power of transgressive tantra for political ends and the justification of violence for enlightenment and serenity. Transgressive tantra are the theologies of esoteric Buddhism which preach rites that transgress social norms and conventions to transcend our profane world into the enlightened and serene sacred world.[7] For aspiring world-conquerors, *cakravartins*, this potential for divinization of their mundane bodies via transgressive tantric rites promised an accumulation of sacred power that could be deployed against their enemies. Parameswara may have visited or spent time at the Majapahit *kraton* in east Java. If so, he would be more vividly aware that nearly a century earlier, Kertanagara, the progenitor of Majapahit, was a practitioner of transgressive tantra and was consecrated as a Jina Buddha under the name Jñānabajra to enhance his prowess for political ends.

In 1275, according to the Majapahit panegyric poem the *Desawarnana/Nāgarakṛtāgama*, canto 41.5, Kertanagara "gave the order to move against the land of Malayu ... and through his divine incarnation, they were defeated".[8] This 1275 Javanese *pamalayu*, or expedition, against South Sumatra would almost certainly still be within the social memory of the people of Palembang and Parameswara a century later. Parameswara may in addition have heard rumours and stories reported in the later Javanese chronicle the *Pararaton*[9] that Kertanagara was assassinated in a palace coup. He may also have been aware that the coup was executed whilst Kertanagara was in the midst of what were "left hand" transgressive Tantra rituals to build up his spiritual-mystical prowess to lead Java and Sumatra in a sacred confederacy against an anticipated Mongol invasion to be launched by Kublai Khan. Kertanagara believed the coming war would be fought on a cosmic level, as Kublai Khan had also been consecrated as a Jina Buddha.[10] Parameswara would also have known that Kertanagara consecrated his father Wisnuwardana as the Bodhisattva Amoghapāśa Lokeśvara with his retinue of Tārā, Sukdhanakumara, Hayagriva and Bhrkuti as a mandala at Candi Jago.[11] In deifying his father as a bodhisattva in monumental form, Kertanagara was making a very public statement about the divinity of Singhasari kingship, which he also embodied and was dedicated to protecting.[12]

More importantly, Parameswara would have been aware that his contemporary, Adityawarman, despatched by the Majapahit court in 1347 to represent them in the Sumatran highlands, had instead declared in Tantric idiom his independence from Majapahit. He appropriated the

Figure 8.1 Candi Jago Amoghapāśa, southwest corner of the temple. The two upper-right hands of the bodhisattva are intact, holding his *amṣmālā*, rosary, and *pāśa*, noose. The upper-left hands still holds a *pustaka*, manuscript, and stalk of a *padma*, lotus. The broken lower-left hands would have held the *kalaśa*, pot of sacred water, and *tridaṇḍi*, the three staves tied together carried by Avalokiteśvara in some of his various forms. The broken two lower-right hands would have been in the gesture, *mudrā*, of reassurance and giving. The tiger pelt is barely visible around the hip of the bodhisattva. (Photo by C.G. Kwa.)

Amoghapāśa statue that Kertanagara had despatched to Sumatra as a symbol of Majapahit domination over the island[13] and moved it to his new centre in the West Sumatra highlands, inscribing on the back of the statue (in a very localized Sanskrit) his claims to the right to protect the people of Melayu as an embodiment of Amoghapāśa.[14]

Figure 8.2 Adityawarman's Amoghapāśa statue from Rambahan, Central Sumatra, which is now in the National Museum, Jakarta. Flanking the bodhisattva are his retinue, Tārā, Sukdhanakumara, Hayagriva and Bhrkuti. Sculptured into the base of the statue are the *saptaratna*, the seven jewels of a world conqueror, *cakravartin*. These are: *aśvaratna* "horse-treasure", *cakraratna* "wheel-treasure", *striratna* "queen/wife-treasure/Lakṣmi", *cintāmaṇi* "thought-jewel", *gehapati* "house-lord/minister", *pariṇāyuaka* "general" and *hastiratna* "elephant-treasure".

Amoghapāśa, in these statues of Kertanagara, is more than the compassionate Bodhisattva unfailingly (*amogha*) capturing sentient beings with his *pāśa*, or "noose, rope", from the sea of illusions to bring them to the shores of enlightenment.[15] In this form the bodhisattva appears to have been the patron saint of Śrīvijaya, as the large number of Amoghapāśa statues in Śrīvijaya statuary from the seventh to the tenth century[16] attest. After which there are no further statues of the bodhisattva until the thirteenth century.

The thirteenth-century Amoghapāśa Lokeśvara enshrined at Candi Jago is, however, about divine kingship and ancestor worship, while the Amoghapāśa shipped to Sumatra is a tantric symbol of power and domination over others. Amoghapāśa's *pāśa* is more than about catching sentient beings to lead them to salvation; it is an auspicious object, an *aṅkuśa*, to catch and bind others in transgressive tantric rites of *ākarṣaṇa* to assert coercive power over them (including divinities).[17] The *Hevajra Tantra*,[18] a central text of esoteric Buddhism widely circulated in Southeast Asia, describes the different rituals for this accumulation of coercive power over others and things.

Within this world of Tantra it is then perhaps not surprising that Parameswara—inspired, if not emboldened, by the precedent of Adityjawarman—elected to symbolize his independence from Majapahit by similarly declaring himself an embodiment of the bodhisattva Amoghapāśa Lokeśvara. He may have done so in an elaborate forty-day ceremony, which the Raffles MS 18 of the *Sulalatus-Salatin* described as an elaborate ritual lustration, or *memandikan*, of Sri Tribuana.[19]

This Raffles MS 18 description of the ceremony appears to correspond to instructions in the *Hevajra Tantra*[20] for a Jar-Consecration (*kalaśābhiṣeka*). The consecration involved the purificatory sprinkling of water to wash away ignorance and initiate the acolyte into the deep knowledge of *prajna*, wisdom. It may have been a consecration ceremony to embody Sri Tribuana as Amoghapāśa Lokeśvara. Tomé Pires, the Portuguese supervisor of the spice trade at Melaka from 1512 to 1515, understood that with this ceremony Parameswara changed his name to "the Great Exempt", or *Mjçura*,[21] the intent of which would not have been lost on his Majapahit overlord.

Parameswara's journey from Palembang to Temasek, which he renamed Singapura, was not because he sighted a lion but because he decided it would be a good place for him to locate his lion-throne—the *siṅhāsana* (Skt.), *singgasana*,[22] which he sat on as a bodhisattva. From Singapura, Parameswara then moved again, arriving first at Muar, which he found inauspicious and so he moved on till he arrived at the mouth of the Bertam River, which he viewed as an auspicious spot for a new port-settlement because his hunting dogs were kicked into retreating by a valiant mouse deer.

Wolters saw the 1436 "genealogist" as seeking to rewrite the contemporary history of Melaka's founding by Parameswara in his alterity as Sri Tribuana, deified as Amoghapāśa Lokeśvara, carrying the legacy of Śrīvijaya to Temasek. Melaka's establishment and rise to success is prefigured in the successful reigns of Sri Tribuana and four generations of successors in Singapura. Both Sri Tribuana and Iskandar Shah left their homeland in Palembang and Singapura to cross the seas or straits in search of locations for new cities. Both sighted valiant animals—the *singha* by Sri Tribuana and the mouse deer by Iskandar Shah—marking an auspicious site for a new settlement. Singapura's rise to become a "great city" under four generations of Sri Tribuana's successors prefigures Melaka's (inevitable) rise under the successors of Iskandar Shah. This rewriting of history to "echo" the past, as Henri Chambert-Loir argues, continues through the entire *Sulalatus-Salatin*, to the fall of Melaka to the Portuguese.[23]

This rewriting of history is not unique to Malay texts. The Dutch linguist C.C. Berg, in a long series of densely argued monographs, has similarly asserted that the Middle-Javanese historical chronicles and texts were written (or re-written) to legitimize and justify the ruler's claim to power and ensure the moral integrity of the realm. These chronicles and texts, including the *Nāgarakṛtāgama* and the *Pararaton*, which historians have read as chronicles of the Javanese past, as the *Sulalatus-Salatin* is of the Malay past, are therefore more history as it should have been written rather than as it has occurred.

Berg has argued[24] that the reigns of the five major kings of Singhasari and Majapahit—Kertanagara, Jayanagar, Rajasanagara and Rajasawardhana—were reinterpreted in the *Nāgarakṛtāgama* and the *Pararaton* as earthly manifestations of the "Fivefold Buddha", the *Pancatathāgata*, to assure the subjects of these east Javanese kingdoms that their earthly existence mirrors that of the spiritual realm of esoteric Buddhism expressed in the architecture of Barabudur built some three centuries earlier. Was the *Sulalatus-Salatin* reference to Sri Tribuana and his four generations of successors a deep trope of Amoghapāśa Lokeśvara and his mandala of four divine attendants ruling Singapura? If so, Melaka's future would have been undoubtedly reassuring when it is prefigured in fourteenth-century Singapura ruled by Iskandar Shah's alterity as Sri Tribuana embodied as Amoghapāśa Lokeśvara with his retinue of Tārā, Sukdhanakumara, Hayagriva and Bhrkuti.

The esoteric Buddhist metaphors and tropes that the 1436 "genealogist" (as Wolters terms him) or narrator could draw upon to construct the origin myth of Melaka and its esoteric Buddhist archetypes would have been within the literary competence of the intended audience in the early decades of fifteenth-century Melaka. They would have understood the deep esoteric Buddhist tropes and figurations referred to, and they would have listened to the narrative for more than its meaning—for an account that would reflect and relate to their own experience and social memories.

But the compiler of the earliest 1612 written text we have of the *Sulalatus-Salatin*, the Raffles MS 18, had to constantly remind his readers that the stories he is telling of Melaka's origins are verifiable and therefore true. The black stone fort of Gelanggui that Raja Shulan overran "still exists to this day", with its name pronounced as "Linggiu".[25] The rock the strongman Badang hurled across Singapore "is there to this day on the extremity of Tanjong Singapura". This suggests that the literary competence of the audience for the 1612 reading of the *Sulalatus-Salatin* had transformed—they had forgotten who Sri Tribuana was.

Classical Malay literature, as Winstedt and Braginsky, among others, have documented, was becoming Islamized. Braginsky[26] has pointed to the emergence of literary self-awareness shaping new genres and genre forms of literature, creative processes and the didactic value of literature. The *Sulalatus-Salatin*, as a political tract, was rewritten within these new modes of literary awareness and in a shifting historical consciousness of the uncertain future of the Johor sultans as they confronted a complex present challenged by Aceh and Luso-Dutch rivalry. The esoteric Buddhist underpinnings of the origin myth of Melaka were forgotten in the new literary awareness defining classical Malay literature in the sixteenth century, which is encapsulated in the doxology at the end of the chapters of the *Sulalatus-Salatin*:

> *WalLahu a'Llamu bissawab wa ilayhil marji'u walmaab*
> (Allah knoweth the Truth. To Him do we return.)

Notes

1. This very speculative note was stimulated by the essays of A. Acri and I. Sinclair in this volume and their other work. It was motivated further by a remarkable Yale NUS College "Capstone Final Report for BA (Honours) in History" by Nicholas Lua Swee Yang, *Tantra below the Winds: The Transgressive King and His Precursors* in AY 2018/19. Lua has attempted to frame the Tantric Buddhist references by Adityawarman, Kertanagara and Jayavarman VII in their statuary and epigraphy to the transgressive sacrality of the tantra in the interplay of mystical power cultivated by these three transgressive kings in their bid for political power in their mundane realms. In attempting this, Lua has read and followed the work of his supervisor Gavin Flood on *The Tantric Body: The Secret Tradition of Hindu Religion* (London: Tauris, 2006). I thank Nicholas Lua for reaching out to me and sharing his essay. This note also draws upon my "Singapura as a Central Place in Malay History and Identity", in *Singapore from Temasek*

to the 21st Century: Reinventing the Global City, edited by Karl Hack and Jean-Louis Margolin, with Karine Delaye (Singapore: NUS Press, 2010), pp. 133–54. I thank Andrea Acri for an appreciative reading of the draft and nuancing my interpretation of Tantra as transgression. I also thank Iain Sinclair for a close reading of a draft of this note and his comments, which I may not have taken full cognizance of. Finally, thanks to Anthony Milner, with whom I first critically read (deconstructed) the *Sejarah Melayu* (as it was then known) in Canterbury in the winter of 1977, for his encouraging comments on this draft.

2. R. Winstedt, *A History of Classical Malay Literature*, rev. ed., reprint no. 12 (Kuala Lumpur: Malaysian Branch of the Royal Asiatic Society, 1989[?]) was first published in 1939 and reprinted several times. Liaw Yock Fang, *A History of Classical Malay Literature*, translated by R. Bahari and H. Aveling (Singapore: Institute of Southeast Asian Studies, 2013) follows a similar historical framing of classical Malay literature.

3. See H.M.J. Maier, *In the Center of Authority: The Malay Hikayat Mereong Mahawangsa*, Studies on Southeast Asia (Ithaca: Cornell University Southeast Asia Program, 1988) on this shift to intertextuality in structuralist and reader-oriented theories of literary analysis of texts.

4. V.I. Braginsky, *The System of Classical Malay Literature*, Koninklijk Instituut voor Taal-, Land- en Volkenkunde working paper 11 (Leiden: KITLV Press, 1993) and elaborated in his *The Heritage of Traditional Malay Literature: A Historical Survey of Genres, Writings and Literary Views* (Leiden: KITLV Press, 2004).

5. Wang Gungwu, "The First Three Rulers of Malacca", *Journal of the Malaysian Branch of the Royal Asiatic Society* 41, no. 1 (1968): 11–22.

6. O.W. Wolters, *The Fall of Śrīvijaya in Malay History* (Kuala Lumpur: Oxford University Press, 1970). Wolters's overarching argument is that the fall of Śrīvijaya and the founding of Melaka, hitherto treated as separate events, are connected.

7. G. Flood, *The Secret Tradition of The Tantric Body: The Secret Tradition of Hindu Religion* (London: Tauris, 2006).

8. Mpu Prapañca, *Deśawarna (Nāgarakṛtāgama)*, translated by S. Robson (Leiden: KITLV Press, 1995), p. 54.

9. *Pararaton (Ken Arok): Het Boek der Koningen van Tumapel en van Majapahit*, edited and annotated by J.L.A. Brandes, 2nd ed. by N.J. Krom. Verhandelingen van her Bataviaasch Genopotschap van Kunsted en Wetenschappen, vol. 42 (The Hague: Nijhoff; Batavia: Albrecht & Co, 1920), p. 80. C.C. Berg (whose work is discussed below) has argued in a series of revisionist studies (which have challenged and infuriated his colleagues) that Kertanagara was a misunderstood empire-builder and that he was working for a sacred confederacy in the *nusantara* built on Kālacakra tantric practices. Berg, "Kertanagara, De Miskende Empirebuilder", *Orientatie* (July 1950): 1–32 and Berg, "Krtanagara's 'Maleise affairs'", *Indonesiē ([Tweemaanelijks] tijdschrift gewijd aan het Indonesisch cultuurebied)* 9 (1956), 386–417.

10. D. Bade, "(Spi)ritual Warfare in 13th Century Asia? International Relations, the Balance of Powers, and the Tantric Buddhism of Krtanagara and Kublilai Khan", in *Esoteric Buddhism in Medieval Maritime Asia: Networks of Masters, Texts, Icons*, edited by A. Acri (Singapore: ISEAS – Yusof Ishak Insitute, 2016), pp. 141–62.

11. See A.R. Kinney, *Worshipping Siva and Buddha: The Temple Art of East Java* (Honolulu: University of Hawai'i Press, 2003), pp. 95–125 for a descriptive interpretation of Candi Jago as a "storybook in stone".

12. K. O'Brien, "Candi Jago as a Mandala", *Review of Indonesian and Malaysian Affairs* 22 (1988): 1–61; 24 (1990), 23–85.

13. N. Reichle, *Violence and Serenity: Late Buddhist Sculpture from Indonesia* (Honolulu: University of Hawai'i Press, 2007), pp. 127–32.

14. H. Kulke, "Adityawarman's Highland Kingdom", in *From Distant Tale: Archaeology and Ethnohistory in the Highlands of Sumatra* (Newcastle upon Tyne: Cambridge Scholars Publishing, 2009), pp. 229–52.

15. The bodhisattva with the "unfailing noose" is one of the some one hundred forms of Avalokiteśvara that was venerated more in Tibet, China, Japan and Southeast Asia than in India, on which, see Lokesh Chandra, *Dictionary of Buddhist Iconography*, Śata-Piteaka Series, vol. 601 (New Delhi: International Academy of Indian Culture/Aditya Prakashan, 1999-), *sub voca* "Amoghapāśa" at pp. 290–309.

16. The tiger pelt worn by Amoghapāśa around his hip is clearly discernable in the Śrīvijaya sculptures illustrated in *The Art of Śrīvijaya*, edited by M.C. Subhadradis Diskul (Kuala Lumpur: Oxford University Press, 1980), most prominently in the bronze statue from Bidor, Perak, illustrated as plate 5 for the chapter on "Śrīvijaya Art in Peninsula Malaysia" at pp. 45ff.

17. D.L. Snellgrove, *Indo-Tibetan Buddhism: Indian Buddhism and their Tibetan Successors* (London: Serindia, 1987, pp. 235–43. I thank Andrea Acri for drawing my attention to this association of the *pāśa* with *ākarṣaṇa* rites.

18. D. Snellgrove, *The Hevajra Tantra: A Critical Study*, 2nd ed. (Bangkok: Orchid Press, 2010), pp. 50–55.

19. *Sejarah Melayu: The Malay Annals, MS Raffles 18, New Romanised Edition*, compiled by Cheah Boon Kheng and transcribed by Abdul Rahman Hj. Ismail, Malaysian Branch of the Royal Asiatic Society reprint no. 17 (Kuala Lumpur: Malaysian Branch of the Royal Asiatic Society, 1998), p. 87.

20. See Snellgrove, *The Hevajra Tantra*, p. 131 for a discussion of the concept of *abhiṣeka* and references to the Sanskrit and Tibetan texts in part 2 of his study.

21. A. Cortesao, trans., *The Suma Oriental of Tomé Pires: An Account of the East, from the Red Sea to Japan, Written in Malacca and India in 1512–1515 and the Book of Francisco Rodrigues: Rutter of a Voyage in the Red Sea, Nautical Rules, Almanack and Maps, Written and Drawn in the East before 1515* (1944; repr., New Delhi: Asian Education Services, 1990), vol. 2, p. 231.

22. *Sejarah Melayu,* Cheah, p. 88.

23. H. Chambert-Loir, "The Sulalat al-Salatin as a Political Myth", *Indonesia* 79 (2005), pp. 131–60.

24. C.C. Berg, "Het Rijk van de Vijfvoudige Buddha", *Verhandelingen der Koninklijke Nederlandse Akademie van Wetenschappen, Aft Letterkunde,* new sers. 69, no. 1 (1962); P. Wheatley, *The Golden Khersonese: Studies in the Historical Geography of the Malay Peninsula before A.D. 1500* (Kuala Lumpur: University of Malaya Press, 1961), p. 304 cites Berg proposing in a lecture to the University of Malaya Historical Society on 29 November 1956 that the etymology of Singapura has to be sought in the esoteric Bhairava-Buddhism of early Majapahit.

25. The search for this black stone fort continues to this day. See Raimy Ćhe-Ross, "The 'Lost City' of Kota Gelanggi: An Exploratory Essay on Textual Evidence and an Excursion into 'Aerial Archaeology'", *Journal of the Malaysian Branch of the Royal Asiatic Society* 77, no. 2 (2004): 27–58. This search for Gelanggi/Linggiu somewhere at the northern shore of what is today the Linggiu reservoir made headline news for several months in the Malaysian media in 2003–4.

26. Braginsky, *Heritage of Traditional Malay Literature,* chap. 4f.

9

Portuguese and Dutch Records for Singapore before 1819: An Overview

Peter Borschberg

This essay aims to provide a synopsis of the different types of sources that are available for the study of the history of Singapore in the period before circa 1800. The objective is not to provide a reconstruction of Singapore history as such, but rather to provide general comments and analyse the sources at hand. This chapter offers an opportunity to step back and share with you the experience I have gathered in identifying, handling and working with different types of sources over the past two decades. In this chapter I will take a closer look at what those different types of sources are able to inform, what their limitations are, and what they generally do not tell us. As the title suggests, the focus of the present exposé is placed on Portuguese and Dutch textual materials broadly defined. This includes manuscript and published sources as well as cartographic specimens that touch on the island of Singapore, its surrounding waters, and the southern stretches of the Malay Peninsula.

Clearly, I am aware that I am not the first to work on these materials, specifically on Portuguese texts. Investigations were already conducted in the 1950s by Ian Alastair Macgregor at the History Department of the University of Singapore.[1] Almost concurrently, Carl Alexander

Gibson-Hill, the former director of the Raffles Museum of Singapore, was studying archaeological evidence, published travelogues and historical cartography.[2] These two researchers made important contributions to the study at that point in time when access to primary sources dating from the early modern period (either in printed form or manuscript) was far more cumbersome and limited than it is today. Much later, in the 1990s, Paulo Pinto published a study, first in Portuguese and later in an updated English translation. He has mined the Portuguese sources to explore the relationship of the Portuguese with Aceh and Johor during the second half of the sixteenth and the opening two decades of the seventeenth centuries. This latter work, however, does not substantially touch on Singapore, and has failed to take into consideration certain Dutch and German language documents from the period under review. Its value is therefore somewhat limited.[3]

Before proceeding, it is appropriate to ask a series of questions that will serve as a guide for the present discussion. These questions are, first, what types of primary sources are there? What is a Portuguese source, or a Dutch one for that matter? Who wrote or drew this source, and what purpose was it meant to serve? What is the source interested in? How many testimonies do we know of and how substantial are they? What are the main challenges arising from the study of historical cartography with reference to Singapore? What does the toponym *Singapura* or any of its many variants mean, and what specifically does it refer to? And, finally, what are the other names for Singapore, the island or the settlement?

Bearing these questions in mind, we now turn to think about what primary sources are at hand for the study of Singapore before the beginning of the nineteenth century. As I have discussed more extensively in an article co-authored with Benjamin Khoo in the *Journal of the Malaysian Branch of the Royal Asiatic Society*, these types of sources fall into four broad categories:[4] first, material objects; in other words, archaeological remains that have been retrieved over the past three decades from archaeological investigations and excavations in and around Singapore. Preliminary investigations have shown that the archaeological finds date primarily from the fifteenth century, though some objects evidently derive from a later period.

As for the second category, we have our texts. These include navigational instructions (such as rutters) and travel reports. The third category is scientific data: for example, evidence of precipitation, droughts, volcano eruptions within the region, or the spread of diseases. The fourth category is cartography. It is evident that not all of these sources are of equal significance for the study of Singapore, and some of them, such as the ones listed under cartography below, offer new and exciting opportunities for researchers, as the recent article by Benjamin J.Q. Khoo entitled "In the Path of the Storms" can testify.[5] This chapter will only address the second and fourth types of evidence; namely, texts and cartographical materials.

Who wrote it, who drew it, and to what end? Answering these questions demands that we know the author of a given source, and further requires us to historicize and contextualize the written materials. One of the most frequently quoted sources is the *Suma Oriental* (Summary of the Orient) by Tomé Pires, which is a treatise that was written in Portuguese in the first quarter of the sixteenth century. Although its importance is without question, this work has its problems. I refer in this instance to the new edition of the Portuguese text prepared by Rui Loureiro in 2016. Other commonly referenced sources are those by the Eurasian cartographer and adventurer Manuel Godinho de Erédia, who, in addition to drawing several important maps of the region (including Singapore), also penned two treatises on the history and culture of the Malay Peninsula. Erédia's works have admittedly come under scrutiny in recent years, and I think here especially of the critical commentaries and introduction written by Jorge Flores, Rui Loureiro and John Everaert.[6] Add to these sources the publication of a hitherto unpublished work, Erédia's *Tratado Ophirico* (Treatise on Ophir) dating from 1616, edited by Juan Gil and the aforementioned Rui Loureiro.[7] It should be noted that the statements encountered in the sources touching on Singapore and the adjacent straits are often confusing and occasionally border on meaningless.

How Do We Classify a Source?

What is a Portuguese source, or even a Dutch source for that matter? We have texts, both published and unpublished, written in an array of European languages including Portuguese, Dutch, German, Spanish, Italian, Latin and others. We are also in possession of certain testimonies written in Asian languages. I think here particularly of the sixteenth-century Ottoman-Turkish rutter *Muhit*, which briefly mentions the geographic location of Singapore, though it is certain that its author referenced this name without ever having been to this part of the world.[8] It should be stated that the materials at hand are often fragmentary, inconclusive and generic. So, then, what makes for a Portuguese or a Dutch source? Is it a question of language? Is it a question of an individual's affiliation? Or does it perhaps depend on the location a given author was working from? Not all the texts known to touch on Singapore and the region dating from before 1800 and affiliated with either the Portuguese or the Dutch have been written in their languages. Consider, for example, John of Empoli's letters, which are in Italian;[9]

the autobiography and memorials of Jacques de Coutre, which are mostly written in Spanish;[10] or the travelogue of Johannes Verken, who worked for the Dutch East India Company (VOC) but wrote his diary in German.[11] The Catholic missionaries, such as Francis Xavier, penned letters in Latin.[12] So should language be the only, or even the decisive, criterion?

Scope and Nature of the Testimonies

How substantial are these written testimonies? My conservative estimate is that there are about one thousand testimonies of varying lengths accessible to researchers in all European languages touching on Singapore and the adjacent straits. The vast majority of these are very short and can range from a few words to a sentence or two. Mentions beyond a paragraph or more in length are rare, with the testimonies of Jacques de Coutre collectively offering the most substantive testimony on Singapore.[13] These more expansive textual fragments are certainly the most malleable and can potentially yield the most useful and substantive information on the region before 1800. The sad fact is, however, that more often than not the written sources do not tell us what we would like them to. I think here particularly of the letters of Jesuit missionary Francis Xavier, which despite being written in Singapore contain no additional information on the region whatsoever. Another example would be John of Lisbon's rutter for the Singapore Straits, which fails to mention the date of the Portuguese destruction of the Singapore settlement.[14] The vast majority of the references touch on natural features such as the waters, the islands, and rarely the *orang laut* who lived in and moved about the waters of the Singapore Straits. These testimonies are often generic and are of little historical value.

In my experience the more substantive testimonies fall into three broad categories. First there is what one could call the testimony of the enthusiast. This is a pearl-string of factoids connected by the word "and". It reminds one of an account of a child returning from a visit to the zoo and explaining excitedly what he has seen. The second type is reminiscent of the account of a disinterested and detached adolescent; again, taking the example of the zoo trip, the adolescent is mainly interested in himself and his friends, and in the things immediately happening around him. The zoo serves only as a backdrop to his focus and interests. The third category is the incidental comment; touching on Singapore is really not the main focus, and a reference is made as an "aside", with little or no detail.

The most substantive sources are those written in Portuguese or in the Dutch language. The question now arises as to how these Portuguese sources stack up in terms of their present-day value to researchers. Context and authorial intentions are key to unlocking the significance of these texts. The Portuguese sources, especially the printed chronicles, celebrate the heroic exploits of the Portuguese officers, mariners and soldiers. These often have a military and sometimes also a commercial focus, or the Portuguese are summarizing stories that probably had been transmitted to them by word of mouth. This is, for example, the case with the story of Parameswara's flight to Singapore and his subsequent founding of Melaka, which one encounters in the *Suma Oriental* (Summary of the Orient) by Tomé Pires, Brás de Albuquerque's *Commentaries of Alfonso de Albuquerque*[15] and the *Décadas da Ásia* (Decades of Asia) by João de Barros.[16] The value of a given document depends not just on the purpose for which a given text was written but also on the author's first-hand familiarity with the situation on the ground as well as on his level of education.

Figure 9.1 Printed portrait of the Portuguese historian João de Barros.

When contrasting the Portuguese sources with the Dutch ones dating from the late sixteenth and early seventeenth centuries, for example, we see that the Dutch faced a very steep learning curve. They were keen to collect as much information about the region as possible. As a trading company, moreover, the Dutch East India Company (VOC) was particularly interested in products for trade, in market mechanisms, taxes, gifts, and a Who's Who of the royal courts, as well as what their enemies—the Portuguese and the Spanish—were getting up to. This desire to collect as much information as possible has resulted in an unexpected level and depth of analysis during the period between approximately 1595 and 1640, which coincides with the Luso-Dutch conflict in the region. This conflict has left us with a substantial paper trail. For reconstructing local conditions (for example of Johor or to a certain extent Singapore) the Dutch sources appear to yield more details. The documentation from VOC channels, moreover, does not erase the agency of the local actors, and readers today will note that the Dutch were willing to concede a considerable degree of agency and autonomy to the Malay rulers or their proxies.

What are the texts interested in? Occasionally I receive phone calls and emails about certain discoveries made by amateurs and professional researchers on the topic of Singapore. When I sit down to have a look at what they have found, I mostly find that they have retrieved some casual remark about the Singapore Straits. In other words, what the sources impart is what could be observed from the deck of a ship passing through the Singapore Straits, or from fetching fresh water on land, such as at Siloso Spring on Sentosa. The large sprawling trees and the thick foliage that are frequently mentioned almost certainly blocked the fuller view that the European observers might have had from the deck of their ship, and what they see therefore is restricted to the immediate coastline or riverbanks. Direct references to a settlement on Singapore exist in Portuguese, Spanish, Dutch and German language texts, but they are problematic in several respects. First, these sources are inconclusive about the size, exact location, or even the level of activity taking place in the port. Nevertheless, a picture emerges from these references that Singapore had a functioning port with a *laksamana* (admiral), and later a *shahbandar* (lord of the haven, harbour master) in the sixteenth and well into the seventeenth centuries.[17]

Cartography and Confusion

I will now turn to explore certain issues arising from historical cartography, both of Singapore Island and the Straits. Anyone who has had a close look at the printed and manuscript charts and maps of the sixteenth, seventeenth and eighteenth centuries will quickly realize that what they have before them is a collage of information that could stem from different periods in history. For example, cartographers would mix information gleaned from Claudius Ptolemy with the latest information from the Age of Discoveries. One is never quite certain how much of the information depicted on a map represents first-hand experience on-site. This problem is further complicated by the fact that we are often confronted with garbled place names, and this is particularly true for the toponym "Singapore", for which there are a range of spellings that are sometimes almost unrecognizable. Cartographers, moreover, were not always sure where a particular city or settlement was located, and Singapore was certainly no exception to this. Sometimes the settlement is placed on the island of Singapore, but sometimes also on the mainland of Johor, which arouses suspicion that Singapore may have been confused with a different place altogether, such as for example Johor Lama in the second half of the sixteenth century.[18]

The confusion put to paper in the charts and maps drawn in Europe during the sixteenth and seventeenth centuries is also reflected in the written texts. It is not always clear what a given toponym actually refers to, and sometimes it is equally unclear where this is exactly located. With specific reference to Singapore, we know that different names and different locations were given over time for the settlement as well as for the island as a whole. For much of the early modern period, the island of Singapore was known as "Pulau Panjang" or in its translation "Long Island". The name "Pullo Polle" found on the maps in Valentijn's landmark publication *Nieuw en Oud Oost-Indië* (New and Old East Indies) seems to be a corruption of the Malay *pulau-pulau* ("many islands" or, liberally, "archipelago"), evidently a reference to Singapore or the adjacent Riau islands.[19] When the name *Sincapura* (or one of its many variant spellings) has been employed, it could be with reference to either the island, the settlement, the port, one of at least two straits (the New and Old Strait), a promontory, coastal range, or in certain Portuguese sources also a "gateway". The French cosmographer André Thevet employed the name Sincapura to include the peninsular hinterland that would correspond more or less to the present-day Malaysian State of Johor.[20] The confusion over what exactly the name *Sincapura* refers to is also reflected in the German encyclopaedia of the mid-eighteenth century published by Johann Heinrich Zedler. In this we find four entries under five different spellings for Singapore.[21] The information contained in this reference work reflects not only the method by which information was compiled, sorted and processed but also what an intelligent and resourceful person proficient in several European languages would be able to find around the first half of the eighteenth century.[22]

Wrap-up and Some Conclusions

In wrapping up this chapter, it is useful to address a couple of additional considerations. The first is the question as to whether there are any more major sources likely to be found? The simple answer is, not in the obvious places. Most of the main archives have been trawled by now and there are probably not many more substantive testimonies to be found in them. The situation with smaller archival holdings, both public and private, is different, and one surmises that any further significant discoveries will probably be found in these. Do the early modern sources contain dark or undisclosed secrets that are just waiting to be discovered? The short answer is, if they do exist, they may not be immediately recognizable as such. That is perhaps because they employ different toponyms that add to the complexity of identifying references.

Moreover, we must recognize and accept that the sources are what they are, with warts and all. They do not necessarily inform us what we would like them to say, they often lack depth, and the authors were perhaps preoccupied with other priorities at the time of writing. One thinks here particularly of John of Empoli's last will and testament, or Francis Xavier's letters written while anchored off Singapore.

Numerically there are more sources for certain periods than for others. The Portuguese sources cover mainly the period 1511–1640, and the Dutch sources for the period from the early seventeenth until the late eighteenth century. Written sources are often difficult to read and even more challenging to understand. Unlocking these depends on the nature and purpose of the text or medium and the level of education of the author or the copyist. The texts are often fragmentary and range from a few words up to a few pages, and the short references form the overwhelming majority. It is not always clear what the toponym *Singapura* refers to, so researchers need to be careful; it can refer to a city or settlement, a port, an island, a promontory, a coastal range, a strait, or a hinterland. Needless to say, a given toponym can also refer to a combination of features. The sources at hand, moreover, offer different explanations of the name *Singapura*. Beyond the "lion city" familiar from the *Sejarah Melayu* (Malay Annals), there are other historically verifiable understandings of the name *Singapura*. The toponym was thought to mean either *falsa demora* (i.e., the wrong or a tricky place to stay), the place where one interrupts one's voyage (*singgah-pura*), or the gateway to the South China Sea (*Cin-gapura*).[23] For the purposes of our historical enquiries and the priorities placed on the information that we require, many (if not most) of the references encountered in the texts can be classified as useless or irrelevant. There are admittedly some more substantial passages of interest, especially in the Dutch materials, but these are clearly the exception.

Notes

1. I.A. Macgregor, "Notes on the Portuguese in Malaya", *Journal of the Malayan Branch of the Royal Asiatic Society (JMBRAS)* 28, no. 2 (1955): 5–47; Macgregor, "Johore Lama in the Sixteenth Century", *JMBRAS* 28, no. 2 (1955): 48–125.

2. C.A. Gibson-Hill, "Singapore Old Strait and New Harbour, 1300–1870", *Memoirs of the Raffles Museum* no. 3 (Singapore: Government Printing Office, 1956). The text of this long article has been republished in Kwa Chong Guan and P. Borschberg, eds., *Studying Singapore before 1800* (Singapore: NUS Press, 2018). See also Gibson-Hill, "Singapore: Note on the History of the Old Straits, 1580–1850", *JMBRAS* 27, no. 1 (1954): 165–214; and Gibson-Hill, "Johore Lama and Other Ancient Sites on the Johore River", *JMBRAS* 28, no. 2 (1955): 126–99.

3.   Paulo Jorge de Sousa Pinto, *Portugueses e Malaios: Malaca e os Sultanatos de Johor e Achém, 1575–1619* (Lisbon: Sociedade Histórica da Independência de Portugal, 1997). The translation appeared as *The Portuguese and the Straits of Melaka, 1575–1619: Power, Trade and Diplomacy* (Kuala Lumpur and Singapore: MBRAS and NUS Press, 2012).

4.   P. Borschberg and Benjamin J.Q. Khoo, "Singapore as a Port City, *c.*1290–1819: Evidence, Frameworks and Challenges", *Journal of the Malaysian Branch of the Royal Asiatic Society* 91, no. 1 (2018): 1–27.

5.   Benjamin J.Q. Khoo, "In the Path of the Storms and 14th Century Singapore. A Portuguese chronicle of the 16th century", *Passage* (May–June), 2018, pp. 12–13. Weather phenomena are also briefly discussed in C.G. Kwa, *Pre-colonial Singapore* (Singapore: Institute of Policy Studies, 2017) and in Derek Heng's contribution to this volume.

6.   M.G. de Erédia, *Informação da Aurea Quersoneso, ou Península, e das Ilhas Auríferas, Carbúculas e Aromáticas,* edited by R.M. Loureiro (Macau: Centro Científico e Cultural de Macau, 2008); Eredia, *Suma de Árvores e Plantas da Índia Intra Ganges,* edited by J.G. Everaert, J.E. Mendes Ferrão, and M. Cândida Liberato (Lisbon: Commissão Nacional para as Comemorações dos Descobrimentos Portugueses, 2001).

7.   M.G. de Erédia, *Tratado Ophirico,* edited and translated by J. Gil and R.M. Loureiro (Macau: Centro Científico e Cultural de Macau and Fundação Jorge Álvares, 2016).

8.   W. Tomaschek, ed. and trans., *Die Topographischen Capitel des Indischen Seespiegels Moḥiṭ* (Vienna: Verlag der Kaiserlich-Königlichen Geographischen Gesellschaft, 1897).

9.   M. Spallanzani, *Giovanni da Empoli: Un mercante fiorentino nell'Asia portoghese* (Florence: Studio per Edizioni Scelte, 1999). Concerning Empoli, see L.A. Noonan, *John of Enpoli and His Relations with Afonso de Albuquerque* (Lisbon: Instituto de Investigação Científica Tropical, 1989).

10. J. de Coutre, *Andanzas asiáticas,* edited by E. Stols, B.N. Teensma, and J. Werberckmoes (Madrid: História 16, 1991). The sections pertaining to Southeast Asia from the autobiography and memorials have been translated into English in Peter Borschberg, ed., *The Memoirs and Memorials of Jacques de Coutre: Security Trade and Society in 17th Century Southeast Asia,* translated by Roopanjali Roy (Singapore: NUS Press, 2013).

11. M. Gotthard Arthus, ed., *Neundter Theil Orientalischer Indien, Darinnen begrieffen Ein kurtze Beschreibung einer Reyse, so von den Holländern unn Seeländern, in die Orientalischen Indien, mit neun grossen und vier kleinen Schiffen unter der Admiralschafft Peter Wilhelm Verhuffen in Jahren 1607, 1608 und 1609 verrichtet worden, neben Vermeldung, was ihnen fürnemlich auff solcher Reyse begegnet unnd zu Handen gangen. Auß kurtzer Verzeichnus Johann Verkens zusammengebracht und in Truck verfertigt durch M. Gotthard Arthus von Dantzig* (Frankfurt: durch Matth. Beckern in Verlegung Iohannis Theodori de Bry, 1612).

12. G. Schürhammer, *Franz Xaver: Sein Leben und seine Zeit*, 4 vols. (Freiburg: Herder Verlag, 1955).

13. P. Borschberg, "Jacques de Coutre as a Source for the Early 17th Century History of Singapore, the Johor River, and the Straits", *Journal of the Malaysian Branch of the Royal Asiatic Society* 81, no. 2 (2008): 71–97.

14. Jacintho I. de Brito Rebello, ed., *Livro de Marinharia. Tratado da Agulha de Marear de João de Lisboa. Roteiros, sondos, e outros conhecimentos relativos á navegação, Codice do século XVI, etc.* (Lisbon: Imprensa Lipanio da Silva, 1903), p. 269; also Luis Jorge R. Semedo de Matos, *Roteiros Portugueses do Extremo Oriente: sua origem e evolução no século XVI* (Lisbon: University of Lisbon Mestrado Dissertation, 2007), p. 72.

15. Tomé Pires, *Suma Oriental: An Account of the East from the Red Sea to Japan. Written in Malacca and India in 1512–1515*, translated and edited by A. Cortesão, 2 vols. (London: Hakluyt Society, 1944); Afonso de Albuquerque, *The Commentaries of the Great A. Dalboquerque, Second Viceroy of India*, translated by Walter de Gray Birch, 4 vols. (London: Hakluyt Society, 1875–95).

16. João de Barros and Diogo do Couto, *Da Ásia, Dos feitos que os Portuguezes fizeram no conquista, e descubrimento das terras e mares do oriente* (Lisbon: Na Regia Officina Typographia, 1778); see also the Dutch translation that also covers the story of the founding of ancient *Singapura* in João de Barros, *Held-dadige Scheeps-togt van Alfonso de Albuquerque na de Roode-Zee In het Jaar 1506, en ervolgens gedaan: behelsende de geleegendheyd, opkomst en voortgang van de Koningrijken Ormuz, Goa, Malacca, etc.* (Leiden: Pieter van der Aa, 1706). John Crawfurd, second Resident of Singapore (1823–26), quotes de Barros for his account of the history of ancient Singapore in his *A Descriptive Dictionary of the Indian Islands & Adjacent Countries* (1856; repr., Kuala Lumpur: Oxford University Press, 1971), p. 402. Iain Macgregor provides an assessment of de Barros (1496–1570) as a historian in his "Some Aspects of Portuguese Historical Writing of the Sixteenth and Seventeenth Centuries on South East Asia", in *Historians of South-East Asia, Historical Writing on the Peoples of Asia*, edited by D.G.E. Hall (London: Oxford University Press, 1961), pp. 179–86, and continuation of his work by Diogo do Couto (1542–1616).

17. Kwa C.G., D. Heng, P. Borschberg, and Tan T.Y., *Seven Hundred Years: A History of Singapore* (Singapore: National Library and Marshall Cavendish, 2019), pp. 79–115; C.G. Kwa, *Singapore Chronicles: Pre-Colonial Singapore* (Singapore: Straits Times Press, 2017).

18. I have previously discussed some of these issues in "Singapura in Early Modern Cartography: A Sea of Challenges", in *Visualising Space. Maps of Singapore and the Region. Collections from the National Archives and National Library of Singapore* (Singapore: National Library Board, 2015), pp. 6–33 and in the opening chapter of Borschberg, ed., *The Singapore and Melaka Straits: Violence, Security and Diplomacy in the 17th Century* (Leiden and Singapore: KITLV Press and NUS Press, 2010).

19. F. Valentijn, *Oud en Nieuw Oost-Indiën, Vervattende Een Naauwkeurige en Uitvoerige Verhandelinge van Nederlands Mogentheyd in de Gewesten, etc.*, 5 parts in 8 vols. (Dordrecht and Amsterdam: Johannes van Braam and Gerard Onder de Linden, 1724–26).

20. A. Thevet, *La Cosmographie Universelle*, 2 vols. (Paris: P. Huillier, 1575), vol. 2, bk. 11, ch. 24.

21. Concerning the Zedler entries, see Borschberg, "Singapore in the Cycles of the Longue Durée", *Journal of the Malaysian Branch of the Royal Asiatic Society* 90, no. 1 (2017): 29–60; Borschberg, "The Singapore Straits in the Latter Middle Ages and Early Modern Period (*c*.13th to 17th Centuries). Facts, Fancy and Historiographical Challenges", *Journal of Asian History* 46, no. 2 (2012): 59–90.

22. Kwa et al., *Seven Hundred Years*, pp. 162–65.

23. Kwa Chong Guan and P. Borschberg, "Singapore's Tricky Place in Archipelagic History", *Straits Times*, 27 October 2018.

10

Zheng He's Navigation Methods and His Visit to Longyamen, Singapore

Tai Yew Seng

At the ISEAS – Yusof Ishak Institute, visitors are greeted by a large wooden engraved navigation chart of Zheng He's voyages displayed on the wall along the corridor, near the front entrance. George Phillips (1836–96), the British Consul at Fuzhou, in Fujian province, published a paper on this navigational chart he found in the book *Wu-pei-pi-shu* 《武备秘书》.[1] He named it Ching Ho's Chart, while J.V.G. Mills called it the Mao Kun Map.[2] The map contains four pages of stellar diagrams and thirty-four places with stellar altitudes, all in India or kingdoms west of India. The Ching Ho Chart/Mao Kun Map is thought to be the earliest Chinese map that depicts Southern Asia, Persia, Arabia and East Africa in an adequate manner, and is particularly important to Singapore as it mentions Danmaxi (Temasek).

How was the map used for navigation? One method to determine the distance a person is standing away from you (commonly used by men who have undergone national service in Singapore) is to stretch out the arm and point the thumb upwards to measure the height of the person. If the person appears about the height of a thumb nail, the distance is approximately a hundred metres. Celestial navigation uses the same principle but measures the stellar altitudes in order to determine location. For example, in order to find the latitude of a position in the Northern Hemisphere, the higher the North Star (Polaris) appears from the horizon, the higher the latitude.

The Stellar Diagram No. 1 (fig. 10.1) depicts the route from Deogarh in India to Hormuz in Persia. In the introduction to Stellar Diagram No. 1 it says:

> Directions for crossing the ocean.
>
> You see the Pei ch'en star [Polaris] is 11 fingers [high, 17° 40′]³, and the Teng lung ku [Crux] is 4.5 fingers [high, 7° 13′].
>
> You see, on the east side, the Chih nü star [Lyra] is 7 fingers [high, 11° 14′]; [this measurement] serves as a base.
>
> You see in the southwest the Pu ssu stars [Fomalhaut?] are 9 fingers [high, 14° 27′], and you see in the northwest the Pu ssu stars [Beta of Pegasus?] are 11 fingers [high, 17° 40′].
>
> Sailing from Ting-te-pa-hsi [Deogarh], on reaching Hu-lu-mo-ssu [Hormuz] you see the Pei ch'en [Polaris] is 14 fingers [high, 22° 29′].⁴

Around the diagram of a three-masted Chinese junk there are eight sets of constellation maps. Each of these has a few small circles linked by thin lines, indicating a constellation. Beside each constellation map it says:

> [On the north]
>
> On crossing the ocean from Ting-te-pa-hsi [Deogarh], the guiding star, the Pei ch'en star [Polaris] is 7 fingers [11° 14′] above the level of the water.⁵
>
> On reaching Sha-ma-ku (Note by Mills: This should be "Sha-ku-ma") Mountain [Jabal Quraiyat], you see the Pei ch'en star [Polaris] is 14 fingers [high, 22° 29′] (Note by Mills: This should be "11 fingers") above the level of the water.
>
> [On the east]
>
> On the east side the Chih nü star [Lyra] is 7 fingers [11° 14′] above the level of the water.
>
> [On the south]
>
> The two stars of Nan mem [Centaurus] are 6 fingers [9° 38′] above the level of the water.
>
> On crossing the ocean from Ting-te-pa-hsi [Deogarh], the Teng lung ku star [Crux] is 8.5 fingers [13° 39′] above the level of the water.
>
> At Sha-ku-ma Mountain [Jabal Quraiyat] the Teng lung ku star [Crux] is 4.5 fingers [7° 13′] above the level of the water.
>
> [On the west]
>
> In the southwest the Pu ssu star [Fomalhaut?] is 9 fingers [14° 27′] above the level of the water.
>
> In the northwest the Pu ssu stars [Beta of Pegasus] are 11 fingers [high, 17° 40′] above the level of the water.⁶

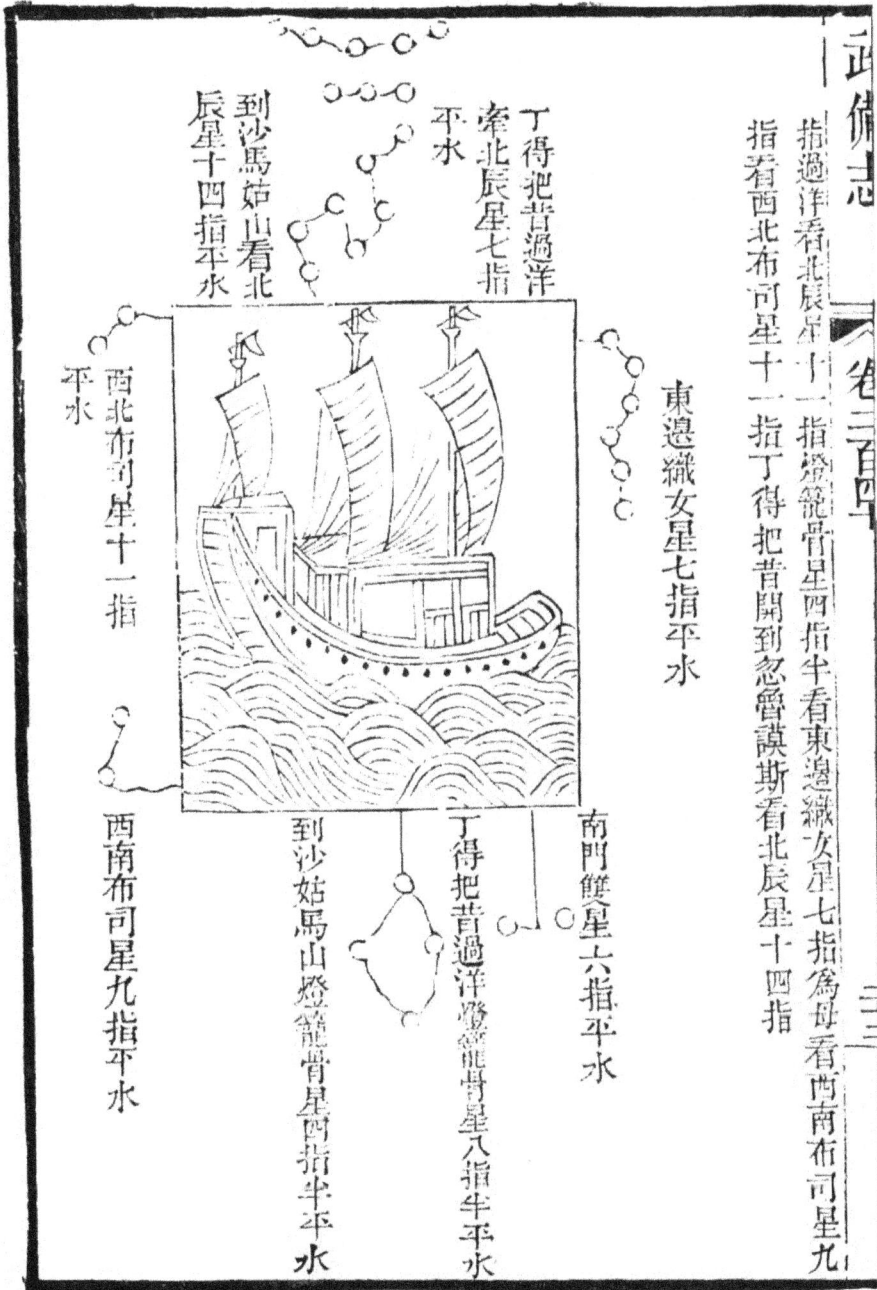

Figure 10.1 Stellar Diagram No. 1 of Mao Kun Map/Ching Ho's Chart. (Credit: Library of Congress.)

As depicted in the Stellar Diagram No. 1, the Mao Kun Map used Polaris, Lyra, Centaurus, Fomalhaut and Beta of Pegasus to guide a ship from Deogarh to Hormuz. The other three stellar diagrams are routes from Ceylon to Kuala Pasai in Sumatra, Poulo Rondo in north Sumatra to Ceylon, and Hormuz in Persia to Calicut in India. None of these diagrams had compass bearings.

Aside from the four stellar diagrams, the stellar altitudes of the Chagos Islands and routes between the Maldives, India, Persia and Mogadishu of Africa are listed on the main map, together with compass bearings. Therefore, even though Chinese navigators did use compass navigation in the Indian Ocean, the evidence suggests that astronomical navigation prevailed. On the other hand, the stellar altitudes were not indicated for the places east of Aceh, Sumatra, Indonesia. The routes from the port of Taicang at the mouth of the Yangtze River, China to Aceh were all given only in compass bearings.

The earliest record of the use of the magnetic compass in maritime navigation is in the book *Pingchow Table Talks* (1119) written by Zhu Yu:

> The captain can recognize the landmarks, observe the stars at night, observe the sun during the day, and during cloudy days, use the south-pointing-needle [i.e., compass]. Or, by using a hundred-foot-rope to bring up the soil of the seabed, he can smell it and will know where [the ship] is.[7]

The Chinese envoy to Korea, Xu Jing (1091–1153), who had written a book entitled the *Illustrated Account of the Xuanhe Embassy to Goryeo*, noted that the compass used on the ship floated on water:

> Tonight, the ship cannot stop in the ocean, therefore one has to observe the stars to move forward. If it is cloudy, the south-pointing-floating-needle is used to indicate the south and north.[8]

These records provide valuable information on ancient navigation. It is known that the Chinese compass used for maritime navigation was used from at least the beginning of the twelfth century and was in the form of a "floating needle". However, Zhu Yu was an observer, not a navigator. Some of his interpretations of navigation practices were wrong. For example, the sailors used the "hundred-foot-rope" not to bring up the soil in order to smell it but to determine the type of sea bed[9] and to measure the depth of the water so as to prevent themselves running aground.

On the Ching Ho Chart/Mao Kun Map, landmarks are indicated along with compass bearings. For example, at the port of Taicang, from which the Chinese fleet set sail, there is an illustration of a temple with the name "Palace of the Celestial Spouse" (fig. 10.2). This is the location where Zheng He erected a stele on 14 March 1431. The stele bore an

Figure 10.2 The Mao Kun Map/Ching Ho's Chart is 220.4 inches long and 8 inches wide. The coastline is not oriented to its true direction and is shown as one line running from right to left. (Credit: Library of Congress.)

inscription that listed his seven expeditions prior to his fleet setting out. For the sailing directions, the map indicated that:

> From Taicang to Wusongjiang: The ship starts from Taicang and steers exactly 105°; after 1 watch (2.4 hours) the ship is level with Wusongjiang.
>
> From Wusongjiang to Nanhuizui: Steers 105°–90°; after 1 watch the ship reaches Nanhuizui and is level with Zhaobaoshan. Exits the port, steers 105°–120°, the water is 16 to 17 feet.[10] (The underlined sections are the present author's additions or corrections to Mills' translation using the original Chinese text.)

The bearings and depth of water are all indicated and the landmarks are illustrated. These are all the information needed. The stellar altitudes are not mentioned.

As shown above, the Mao Kun Map indicates that there were two different navigation traditions for the Pacific and Indian Ocean. As the Chinese were familiar with the Pacific, they may have primarily used the compass for navigation. However, when they entered the Indian Ocean, aside from using the compass, it is likely that they employed Indian or Persian pilots for navigation. This would not be unusual. When the Portuguese explorer Vasco da Gama (1460s–1524) first circumvented the southern tip of Africa in 1498, for example, he employed an Indian pilot in Malindi to guide the expedition to Calicut (Kozhikode), India. This may have been a common practice in the fifteenth century.

The methods of astronomical navigation and compass navigation were later developed into the use of the sextant to take the altitudes, and this allowed maps to be navigated with greater accuracy. These methods survived until the use of the Global Positioning System for navigation dominated, in the late twentieth and twenty-first century.

Zheng He Navigation and Singapore

Ancient Singapore, or Longyamen, is mentioned in Wang Dayuan's *Description of the Barbarians of the Isles* (1350) and *The Yuan Dynasty History* (1370). There is a different toponym—Lingyamen—in Zhao Rukuo's *A Description of Barbarous Peoples* (1225). Hirth and Rockhill[11] cited Groeneveldt (1880/1887) to suggest that Lingyamen is the Lingga Straits and Island. In 1915, W.W. Rockhill[12] cited Warren D. Barnes (1911) to suggest that Longyamen is the Singapore Strait. This differentiated Longyamen from Lingyamen. Some researchers have adopted his suggestion. In 1961, Hsu Yun Tsiao pointed out that Lingyamen and Longyamen are the same location.[13] This problem can be resolved by comparing the language variations used in China. Zhao Rukuo, who was a native of Taizhou, Zhejiang, spoke Wuyu. Wang Dayuan who was a native of Nanchang, Jiangxi, spoke Ganyu. They were in Quanzhou, where the natives spoke Minyu (Hokkien). When they translated the toponym Leng-ga, used by Minyu sailors, their language background influenced the choice of the Chinese characters they used. With this in mind, we know that Zhao Rukuo transcribed the toponym as Ling-ya and Wang Dayuan transcribed it as Long-ya. Table 10.1 shows the transcription of Singapore, Langkasuka and Langkawi, which consistently match the language variety each writer spoke.

Ships from Quanzhou port, then the busiest port in the world according to Marco Polo (1254–1324) and Ibn Baṭūṭah (1304–77), traded one third of their goods at Longyamen before heading to Sri Vijaya and other ports. This is an indication of the huge volume of trade carried on in ancient Singapore. Located at the cross-junction of the maritime trade road, it was inevitable that when Emperor Ming Chengzu (r. 1403–24) sent Zheng He to the Indian Ocean, he would sail through Longyamen. The folios 15 and 15v of the chart recorded the course of navigation, with compass bearings from Jilimen (Karimun Island) to Baijiao (Pedra Branca) through Longyamen, which the fleet sailed through on their way back from the Indian Ocean. It is translated as follows:

> [Fig. 10.3] From Jilimen (Karimun), for 5 watches the ship steers 112.5°, then 120°, makes Changyao Isle to exit Longyamen. From Longyamen, steers 82.5° for 5 watches, the ship makes Baijiao (Pedra Branca).[14]

From the north of Karimum Island to Changyao Isle, the compass bearing is 112.5°, followed by 120°. At this point the course changes from southeast to northeast. In 1970, Mills suggested that this turning point is Pulau Satumu or Raffles Lighthouse. This indicates that the Zheng He fleet passed the Main Strait to Pedra Branca without entering Keppel Bay. Lin Wo Ling suggested that the ships from the west went southwards to Lingga Island, and the strait is the northern entrance of Riau Strait between Bintan and Batam.[15] Maritime engineer Chung Chee Kit argued that Lin Wo Ling overestimated the speed of ancient

Location	Zhao Rukuo	Wang Dayuan	Minyu/Hokkien (Amoy)
(Singapore)	Ling-ya-men 凌牙门	Long-ya-men 龙牙门	Leng-ga-mng/ Leng-ga-mng
Langkasuka	Ling-ya-si-jia 凌牙斯加	Long-ya-xi-jiao 龙牙犀角	Leng-ga-su-ka/ Leng-ga-se-kak
Langkawi	n.a.	Long-ya-pu-ti 龙牙菩提	n.a./ Leng-ga-po-theh

Table 10.1 Comparison of toponyms in Minyu/Hokkien as transcribed by Zhao Rukuo and Wang Dayuan.

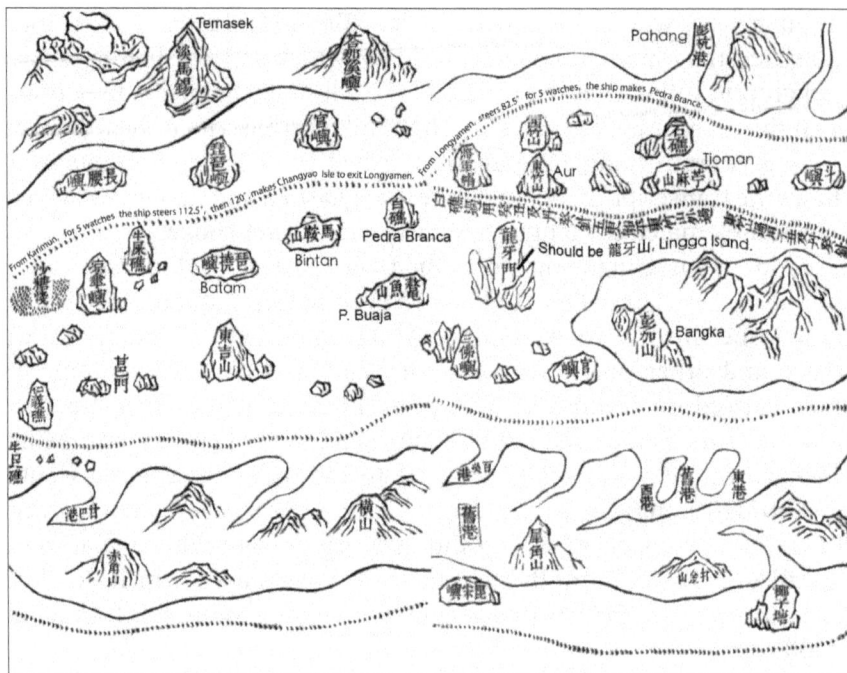

Figure 10.3 Folios 15 and 15v of the Ching Ho Chart show the compass bearings from Karimun Island to Pedra Branca. (Credit: Library of Congress.)

ships, which caused him to come to a wrong conclusion.[16]

There is evidence to show that Zheng He's fleet did visit Longyamen. *The Overall Survey of the Star Raft* (1436) by Fei Xin is the official document presented to the emperor in 1435. In comparison to the documents by Ma Huan (1416/1451) and Gong Zhen (1434), this is the official version of Zheng He's expedition. The document deserves more attention, particularly the record of the fleet's visit to Singapore; but, sadly, important information in these documents has been overlooked by researchers.

In the preface to *The Overall Survey of the Star Raft*, Fei Xin mentions that the places listed in part two were not visited by him:

> 信年始十四，代兄当军……年至二十二，永乐至宣德间，选往西洋，四次随征。正使太监郑和等至诸海外，历览诸番人物风土所产，集成二峡，曰《星槎胜览》。前集者亲监目识之所至也，后集者采辑传译之所实也。

> When I was fourteen years old, [I] took my elder brother's place in the army.... When [I was] twenty-two years old, during the reign of Yongle [1403–24] and Xuande [1426–35], [I was] selected four times for Indian Ocean expeditions. [I] followed the envoy Zheng He and his colleagues on trips overseas, experienced foreign customs and products, recorded

them in two parts entitled *The Overall Survey of the Star Raft*. The first part is a record of what I personally experienced and saw at the locations, the second part is a selection and edition of translator records.[17]

Because he declared that part two of his book was adapted from translators, some researchers concluded that Zheng He did not visit Singapore in the early fifteenth century. Fei Xin had stated that he was selected four times for the Indian Ocean expeditions, which were conducted in the years 1409, 1412, 1416 and 1430. This means he was not involved in the four other major expeditions (1405, 1407, 1421 and 1424) conducted by the Ming dynasty. Furthermore, Fei Xin had clearly stated that part two was taken from information collected by his translator colleagues. A comparison of *The Overall Survey of the Ocean's Shores* (1416/1451) by Ma Huan and *Gazetteer of the Barbarian Countries in the Western Oceans* (1434) by Gong Zhen shows there are similarities in the accounts. This is because the information was from the same sources—the records of the translators. Part two of Fei Xin's book did use some information from *Description of the Barbarians of the Isles* (1350); for example, the description of Longyamen. However, it should be noted that Wang Dayuan's *Description of the Barbarians of the Isles* (1350) recorded ninety-nine countries. So why did Fei Xin only select a few of the places recorded there? One reason could be that he was trying to impress upon the reader that the recorded locations, both in part one and part two, were kingdoms the Ming envoys had visited.

In part two of Fei Xin's book, three locations are mentioned— Giumbo, Mogadishu and Brawa—that are located along the east coast of Africa. These places are not mentioned in the works of Ma Huan, Gong Zhen or Wang Dayuan. These were not the usual destinations of Chinese traders, and probably only Zheng He's fleet had brought the Chinese there. These locations listed in part two show that Fei Xin has tried to give his readers a fuller perspective of the Indian Ocean expeditions by listing the names of the kingdoms that the Ming envoys had visited, even though they were not recorded in other writings.

A comparison of the works of Fei Xin with those of Ma Huan, Gong Zhen and Wang Dayuan reveals something else very unusual. Each of the records in *The Overall Survey of the Star Raft* (1436) ended with a poem. These did not attract the attention of researchers, and at least one of them considered them "not interesting".[18] J.V.G. Mills did a full translation of *The Overall Survey of the Star Raft* (1436) without publishing it. Roderich Ptak annotated and edited the translation of Mills. When he published it in 1996, the editor deleted all the poems.[19] With this dismissal of the poems by Fei Xin, an important piece of evidence related to the visits by Zheng He's fleet to Singapore in the early fifteenth century was omitted. The record on Longyamen, Ancient

Singapore, has this poem at the end of the passage:

山峻龙牙状，中通水激湍。
居人为掳易，番舶往来难。
入夏常多雨，经秋且不寒。
从容陪使节，到此得游观。

The hills are high and steep and appear as dragon's teeth; between them,
      a strong current of water passes through.
The people are adept at piracy, the foreign ships pass through with
      difficulty.
It is rainy in the summer, warm through the autumn.
Leisurely accompanying the envoy, [we are] able to tour and sightsee
      here.

The first six sentences of the poem repeat the prose content mainly adopted from Wang Dayuan's account of the two hills the ships sailed between at the west entrance of Keppel Bay. The Chinese name of Longyamen refers to Batu Berlayer, which looked like giant canine teeth sticking out of the water. It was also the official name of ancient Singapore in the *Yuan Dynasty History*. The seventh and eighth sentences are significant. They describe the envoy of the Ming dynasty Indian Ocean mission making an excursion into ancient Singapore. The ship may have stopped to be replenished and the ship's commanders and envoy could have landed to explore a part of early fifteenth century Singapore. They were probably at the site of Temasek city, not Keppel Bay. The last two sentences use the words "leisurely" and "sightseeing", which may indicate a peaceful and scenic environment. The phrase "you guan" (游观) was used by Po Chü-i/Bai Jüyi (772–846) in his *Number Ninth of the Sequel of Ten Old Poems* (《续古诗十首 • 其九》), which describes him "holding up his robes to walk around and explore the woods and the streams". This is quite different from the repeated descriptions and comments on piracy in the writings of Wang Dayuan.

By this time, Parameswara had fled to Malacca and established the Melaka Kingdom. Longyamen had aligned with Siam and was no longer at war with it. There was half a century of peace until the Melaka Kingdom started to expand to the south in the mid-fifteenth century and expelled Siam from Pahang, Johor and Singapore. This was a peaceful period for Longyamen.

In the second sentence of the poem, it was recorded that there was a very strong current at the passage. This piece of information was not mentioned in Wang Dayuan's *Description of the Barbarians of the Isles* (1350). As naval officers on board, Fei Xin's colleagues must have observed the speed of the current when they entered the narrow passage. On the other hand, the Ching Ho Chart/Mao Kun Map indicates that from the north of Karimun Island the Chinese ships steered towards the Changyao Isle, or "Long Waist Isle". Sentosa Island was called Pulo

Panjang, or "Long Island", according to a letter written by Bonham in October 1842.[20] The coastal area of Singapore Island west of Sentosa is Pasir Panjang, or Long Beach. At Pasir Panjang there are strong currents that bring ships straight to the west entrance of the Longyamen.[21] There are some very detailed records by the Portuguese and British of how to navigate through the Selat Sembilan between the Jurong Islands and Singapore Island to Keppel Bay. Later Chinese rutters of the seventeenth century only warned the navigator not to sail through the passage at night, probably because of the strong current and the reefs.

Conclusion

Chinese navigators have used the compass on ships from at least the early twelfth century. When they entered the unfamiliar waters of the Indian Ocean they employed pilots with local knowledge to navigate. According to the four pages of stellar diagrams in the Ching Ho Chart/ Mao Kun Map, Zheng He's fleets used stellar altitudes to determine their locations from Aceh to India, the Middle-East and Africa. But when they were back in Southeast Asia and East Asia, they would shift their navigation mode to the use of compass bearings.

The Chart indicates that Zheng He's fleet passed through Longyamen using compass bearings. A question arises as to whether Zheng He visited Singapore if his fleet sailed through the Main Strait, which Mills suggested. By analysing the locations mentioned in Fei Xin's book and the poem that ended each record, it can be concluded that the Zheng He fleet did visit Longyamen, Ancient Singapore.

Acknowledgements

I would like to thank *NSC Highlights* editor Foo Shu Tieng for her suggestions and help in the editing of an early version of this paper, Kwa Chong Guan for inviting me to contribute it and his valuable input regarding the structure of the paper, and Nelly Kwa for editing the second version of this paper. I would like to thank my colleague at Temasek History Research Centre Michael Flecker for giving feedback on navigational practices. This paper would not have been written without their encouragement and sharing.

Notes

1. George Phillips, "The Seaports of India and Ceylon", *Journal of the North China Branch of the Royal Asiatic Society,* n.s. 21 (1886): 30–42.

2. J.V.G. Mills, *Ma Huan: Ying-yai Sheng-lan 'The Overall Survey of the Ocean's Shores',* 1433 (Cambridge: Cambridge University Press, 1970), p. 236.

3. Something is missing before the first sentence in the original map. The full introduction should read: "Map of the guiding stars when crossing the ocean in travelling from Ting-te-pa-hsi [Deogarh] to Hu-lu-mo-ssu

[Hormuz]. From Ting-te-pa-hsi [Deogarh], the Pei ch'en star [Polaris] is 7 fingers [11° 14′], coming to Sha-ku-ma [Jabal Quraiyat Mountain] you see the Pei ch'en star [Polaris] is 11 fingers [high, 17° 40′]", and the following sentences.

4. Mills, *Ma Huan*, p. 337.

5. The Ting-te-pa-hsi [Deogarh] has the same latitude as Kuli [Calicut/Kozhikode] in the fourth stellar diagram that indicates the return route from Hormuz to India. Therefore, Mills is giving the latitude of Calicut (Kozhikode).

6. Mills, *Ma Huan*, p. 337–38.

7. 朱彧《萍洲可谈》[Zhu Yu, *Pingchow Table Talks*] (Beijing: Zhonghua Publishing, 2007), p. 133.

8. 徐兢《宣和奉使高丽图经》文渊阁四库全书 [Xu Jing, "Illustrated Account of the Xuanhe Embassy to Goryeo", in *Wen Yuan Ge Si Ku Quan Shu*], vol. 593 (1123; repr., Taipei: Commercial Press, 1986), p. 895.

9. Personal communication with Michael Flecker.

10. Mills, *Ma Huan*, p. 261.

11. Friedrich Hirth and W.W. Rockhill, *Chau Ju-Kua: His Work on the Chinese and Arab Trade in the Twelfth and Thirteenth Centuries, Entitled Chu-fan-chï* (St Petersbrug: Imperial Academy of Science, 1911; repr., Taipei: Ch'eng Wen Publishing Company, 1967), p. 64.

12. W.W. Rockhill, "Notes on the Relations and Trade of China with the Eastern Archipelago and the Coast of the Indian Ocean during the Fourteenth Century, Part II", *T'oung Pao*, 2nd ser. 16, no. 1 (March 1915): 129.

13. 许云樵《马来亚史》[Hsu Yun Tsiao, *History of Malaya*] (1961; repr., Singapore: Youth Book, 2006), p. 92.

14. Mao Yuanyi, Map, in *Wu Bei Zhi, juan* 240 (China: 1621), folios 15v and 15, http://hdl.loc.gov/loc.gmd/g7821rm.gct00058.

15. Lin Wo Ling, *Long Ya Men Xin Kao* (Singapore: Nanyang Xuehui, 1999).

16. Chung Chee Kit, "Longyamen is Singapore: The Final Proof", in *Admiral Zheng He and Southeast Asia*, edited by Leo Suryadinata (Singapore: Institute of Southeast Asian Studies, International Zheng He Society, 2005), p. 142–68.

17. 马欢著，冯承钧校注《瀛涯胜览校注》[Ma Huan, *The Overall Survey of the Ocean's Shores*, annotated by Feng Chengjun] (Beijing: Zhonghua Publishing House, 1954).

18. Paul Pelliot, "Les grands voyages maritimes chinois au début du XVe siècle", *T'oung Pao*, 2nd ser. 30, nos. 3/5 (1933): 329.

19. Fei Hsin, *Hsing-ch'a Sheng-lan: The Overall Survey of the Star Raft*, translated by J.V.G. Mills and revised and annotated by Roderich Ptak (Wiesbaden: Harrassowitz, 1996), p. 21.

20. C.A. Gibson-Hill, "Singapore: Notes on the History of the Old Strait, 1580–1850", *Journal of the Malayan Branch of the Royal Asiatic Society* 27, no. 1 (May 1954): 183.

21. Warren D. Barnes, "Singapore Old Straits and New Harbour", *Journal of the Straits Branch of the Royal Asiatic Society* 60 (1911): 27.

Bibliography

This bibliography is in two parts. The first part lists the transcriptions and translations of the significant primary texts quoted by contributors to this volume. The second part lists the major studies cited by contributors.

Primary Texts, Listed by Title

"The Malay Annals or Sejarah Melayu: The Earliest Recension from MS. No. 18 of the Raffles Collection in the Library of the Royal Asiatic Society, London", edited by R.O. Winstedt. *Journal of the Malayan Branch of the Royal Asiatic Society* 16, no. 3 (1938): 1–226.

"Sějarah Mělayu or 'Malay Annals', A Translation of Raffles MS 18 (in the Library of the R.A.S., London)", translated with commentary by C.C. Brown. *Journal of the Malayan Branch of the Royal Asiatic Society* 25, nos. 2–3 (1952): 5–276.

Sejarah Melayu or "Malay Annals", translated by C.C. Brown, with new Introduction by R. Roolvink. Kuala Lumpur: Oxford University Press Historical Reprints, 1970.

Sejarah Melayu: The Malay Annals; MS. Raffles No. 18, New Romanised Edition, compiled by Cheah Boon Kheng, romanised by Abdul Rahman Haji Ismail. Reprint No. 17. Kuala Lumpur: Malaysian Branch of the Royal Asiatic Society, 1998.

Malay Annals, translated by C.C. Brown. Reprint No. 28. Kuala Lumpur: Malaysian Branch of the Royal Asiatic Society, 2009.

Pararaton (Ken Arok): Het Boek der Koningen van Tumapel en van Majapahit, edited and annotated by J.L.A. Brandes, 2nd ed. by N.J.

Krom. Verhandelingen van her Bataviaasch Genopotschap van Kunsted en Wetenschappen, no. 42. The Hague: Nijhoff; Batavia: Albrecht & Co, 1920.

The Pararaton: A Study of the Southeast Asian Chronicle, translated by I. Gusti Putu Phalgundi. New Delhi: Sundeep Prakashan, 1996.

Het Oud-Javaansche Lofdicht Nāgarakṛtāgama van Prapañca (1365 AD), translated by H. Kern, annotated by N.J. Krom. The Hague: Nijhoff for Koninklijk Instituut voor Taal-, Land- en Volkenkunde, 1919.

Java in the 14th Century: A Study in Cultural History, The Nagara-Kĕrtāgama by Rakawi *Prapañca of Majapahit, 1365 A.D.,* 3rd ed. by T.G.Th. Pigeaud. Koninklijk Instituut voor Taal-, Land- en Volkenkunde. The Hague, Nijhoff, 1960–63, 5 volumes.

Deśawṇana (Nāgarakṛtāgama) by Mpu Prapañca, translated by Stuart Robson. Verhandelingen van het Koninklijk Instituut voor Taal-, Land- en Volkenkunde 169. Leiden: KITLV Press, 1995.

Kakawin Dēśa Warṇnana uthawi Nāgara Kṛtāgama: Masa keemasan Majapahit, translated by I. Ketut Riana. Jakarta: Penerbit Buku Kompas, 2009.

赵如适著，杨博文校释《诸蕃志校释》 [*Zhufan zhi jiaoshi,* by Zhao Rukuo, edited by Yang Bowen]. Beijing: Zhonghua shu ju chu ban she, 1996.

Chau Ju-kua: His Work on the Chinese and Arab Trade in the Twelfth and Thirteenth Centuries, entitled Chu-fan-chi, translated and annotated by Friedrich Hirth and W.W. Rockhill. 1911; repr., New York: Paragon Book Reprint Corp, 1966; repr., Taipei: Ch'eng Wen Publishing Company, 1967.

汪大渊著，苏继廎校释《岛夷志略校释》 [*Daoyi   zhilue   jiaoshi* by Wang Dayuan, edited and annotated by Su Jiqing]. Beijing: Zhonghua shu ju, 2000.

Daoyi zhilue jiaoshi translated. "Notes on the Relations and Trade of China with the Eastern Archipelago and the Coasts of the Indian Ocean during the Fourteenth Century", by W.W. Rockhill. *T'oung Pao,* 2nd ser. 15 (1914): 419–47; 16 (1915): 61–159, 236–71, 374–92, 435–67, 604–26.

万明《明钞本〈瀛涯胜览〉校注》 [*Ming chaoben "Yingyai shenglan" jiaozhu,* by Ma Huan, edited by Wan Ming]. Guangzhou: Guangdong renmin chubanshe, 2018.

Ma Huan, Ying-yai Sheng-lan, *The Overall Survey of the Ocean's Shores* [1433], translated and edited by J.V.G. Mills. Hakluyt Society, Extra Series no. 42. Cambridge: University Press for Hakluyt Society, 1970.

费信《星槎胜览》 [*Xincha Shenglan Jiaozhu*, by Fei Xin], edited and annotated by Feng Cheng Jun. Changsha: Commercial Press, 1938.

Hsing-ch'a Sheng-lan: The Overall Survey of the Star Raft by Fei Hsin, translated by J.V.G. Mills, revised, annotated and edited by Roderick Ptak. Wiesbaden: Harrassowitz Verlag, 1996.

The Suma Oriental of Tomé Pires: An Account of the East, from the Red Sea to Japan, written in Malacca and India in 1512–1515 and The Book of Francisco Rodrigues, Rutter of a Voyage in the Red Sea, Nautical Rules, Almanack and Maps, Written and Drawn in the East before 1515, translated and edited by Armando Cortesão, 2 vols. Hakluyt Society, 2nd sers. 39 and 40. London: Hakluyt Society, 1944; repr., New Delhi: Asian Educational Services, 1990.

A Suma Oriental de Tomé Pires e o Livro de Francisco Rodrigues, edited by Armando Cortesão. Coimbra: Por Ordem da Universidade, 1978.

Suma Oriental, by Tomé Pires, edited by Rui Manuel Loureiro. Lisbon: Centro Científico e Cultural de Macau and Fundação Jorge Álvares; Macau: Fundação Macau, 2017.

Analytical Studies

Andaya, L.Y. *The Kingdom of Johore 1641–1728: Economic and Political Developments.* Kuala Lumpur: Oxford University Press, 1975,

———. *Leaves of the Same Tree: Trade and Ethnicity in the Straits of Melaka.* Honolulu: University of Hawai'i Press, 2008.

Braginsky, V.I. *The Heritage of Traditional Malay Literature: A Historical Survey of Genres, Writings and Literary Views.* Leiden: KITLV Press/ Singapore: Institute of Southeast Asian Studies, 2004.

Gibson-Hill, C.A. "Singapore: Note on the History of the Old Straits, 1580–1850". *Journal of the Malayan Branch of the Royal Asiatic Society* 27, no. 1 (1954): 165–214.

———. "Singapore Old Strait and New Harbour, 1300–1870". *Memoirs of the Raffles Museum* 3. Singapore: Government Printing Office, 1956, pp. 11–115. Reprinted in Kwa and Borschberg, *Studying Singapore before 1800*, pp. 221–308.

Kwa, C.G., and P. Borschberg, eds., *Studying Singapore before 1800.* Singapore: NUS Press, 2018.

Miksic, J.N. *Singapore and the Silk Road of the Sea, 1300–1800.* Singapore: NUS Press, 2013.

Wheatley, P. *The Golden Khersonese: Studies in the Historical Geography of the Malay Peninsula before* A.D. *1500.* Kuala Lumpur: University of Malaya Press, 1961.

Wolters, O.W. *The Fall of Śrīvijaya in Malay History.* London: Lund Humphries; Kuala Lumpur: Oxford University Press, 1970.

Index

Page references in bold refer to figures. Numbers prefixed by "n" refer to notes.

www.ingramcontent.com/pod-product-compliance
Lightning Source LLC
Chambersburg PA
CBHW050404110426
42812CB00006BA/1799

* 9 7 8 9 8 1 4 9 5 1 1 1 1 *